MW01613264

KINGDOM RULES

Seven Conversations

David Udom

CHAINBREAKER

PUBLISHING

Copyright 2013 by David Udom

Kingdom Rules: Seven Conversations
by David Udom

Printed in the United States of America

ISBN 978-0-9777532-2-2 Paperback Edition

Library of Congress Control Number: 2013935051

All rights reserved solely by the author. The author guarantees all contents are original and do not infringe upon the legal rights of any other person or work. No part of this book may be reproduced in any form without the permission of the author. The views expressed in this book are not necessarily those of the publisher.

Unless otherwise indicated, Bible quotations are taken from The King James Version of the Holy Bible.

Chainbreaker Publishing
611 Potomac Place, Ste. 105
Smyrna, Tennessee
TN 37167. (615) 459-6855

Produced by Pedernales Publishing, LLC
www.pedernalespublishing.com

Cover by John Zercher

Contents

FOREWORD

I have discovered in nearly twenty years of preaching the Gospel and fifteen years of pastoring God's people that it is not necessarily the mile of the word, it's the meat in the word that makes a lasting difference. What I mean is that long words certainly have their place in dissertations and academic discourse, but meaningful words undeniably occupy a significant place in helping people go the distance in this course we call life. While the mile word is impressive to the ear, the meat word leaves an impression in the heart and mind of the hearer.

In his new labor of love, David Udom presents us—the readers—with a meal that tastes good and is good for us at the same time. Not only is his approach to Christian maturity easily digested, the truthfulness of his words is able to provide us nourishment for the long haul.

Let's face it, living the life of a believer is not exactly what some of us had been told prior to our coming to the Lord. Many of us were taught that if we gave our hand to the preacher and our heart to God, everything would be alright. However, we later discovered that we had more questions after conversion than we ever had before. To top it off, we learned that others who had experienced conversion before us still had unanswered questions just like us and ours.

In *Kingdom Rules: Seven Conversations*, Brother Udom carefully and lovingly caters to the needs that so many of us have. He provides answers to questions that we have already asked and even have yet to ask. That's the power of this book, in a nutshell. What Brother Udom offers to us in this book is a real contribution to our understanding of who God is and what His purpose is for each of us in His Kingdom.

So, do yourself a favor, and dig in. You are going to enjoy and be blessed!

Pastor Vincent Windrow,
Olive Branch Missionary Baptist Church
Antioch/Murfreesboro, Tennessee.

AUTHOR'S NOTE

This book is written primarily for the believer. My first volume in the Kingdom series, *Kingdom Come: A Book of Threes* was written primarily for the unbeliever bold and curious enough to seek for the truth about God, and about us.

This book is for those who found what they were looking for. But this is a new journey, and with it comes a fresh set of challenges. If they are anything like me, they have a lot of new questions.

Kingdom Rules: Seven Conversations is a modest attempt at answering those questions. It starts off on Day One with the convert speaking, straight talk from the heart, with no guile. From his lips to God's ears, he asks God about the challenges he faces.

God answers. In seven sections, I depict God answering the questions put to him with grace, patience and clarity. As is so often the case, God tenders these answers through the voices of other people.

So let's travel to God's kingdom together, in discovery and brotherly love.

Happy reading.

David Udom.
February 21, 2013

DAY ONE

"So, what exactly am I supposed to do now?"

"Who is Jesus Christ exactly? I mean, really?"

"God, it's hard to walk with you. Every step seems to get me rejected by the world!"

"I don't think I'm good enough for you, God. I'm too flawed."

"Okay, I'm finally becoming somebody! What comes next?"

"Will I also be judged, now that I've gotten my act together?"

"Sometimes I just don't know how to show my love for you, God. How do I show you my love?"

THE FEAR OF THE LORD

*Hearken unto me: I will teach you
the fear of the LORD. Psalm 34:11.*

Chapter 1

In most circles, fear is a dirty word.

No one wants to be really afraid. I'm not talking about the short-lived "fun" fear, of horror movies. That is not true fear. Movie fear mixes far too well with Pepsi and popcorn to be the real thing. Besides, it usually disappears once you leave the movie theater.

I'm talking about the kind of fear that you don't turn off by walking out of a room and excitedly discussing it with your friends. I'm talking about the paralyzing, "I'm afraid to admit I had it" fear. No one likes that.

So, we probably can all relate when I say it's hard to know what to do with the very next statement I'm about to make.

The fear of the Lord is the beginning of wisdom. Psalm 111:10.

Is this statement true? It comes from the Holy Bible, that sacred life manual of all Christians which, in my eyes at least, makes it true. And yes, at first glance this statement doesn't seem to make any sense.

Fear God? I thought I was supposed to love him, not fear him! And wouldn't happiness be a better starting point for wisdom? I rather like happy, it makes me feel complete. Fear makes me feel…*small*. You don't need to be a rocket scientist to figure out which word I'd rather make friends with.

So for me, and I dare say for most people, the fear word creates problems. Is it possible that the word translated "fear" from the original ancient Hebrew and Greek texts of the Bible actually means respect, regard or reverence? Maybe one of these "respectful" words is a capable substitute, wherever fear is used in Bible scriptures.

Respect, regard, and reverence occur seventy-nine times in the Bible, in many instances instructing us to respect God. Only *two* out of those seventy-nine instances used a word that could be interpreted as fear! Obviously, the ancient Hebrews and Greeks understood respect, reverence and regard, and almost always used them in a different context from fear.

Fear and afraid are used six hundred and seven times. The Greeks used versions of the Greek word "phobos," from which we get the English language word "phobia." I do not respect my phobias, I fear them. Two Hebrew words make up the vast majority of the words translated to fear, two remarkably consistent words, one being an extreme version of the other. The same Hebrew word for fear in "the fear of the Lord" is used in the following passage:

> *Yea, though I walk through the valley of the shadow of death, I will fear no evil. Psalm 23:4.*

The same word is translated to fear in this quote,

Sanctify the LORD of hosts himself; and let him be your fear, and let him be your dread. Isaiah 8:13.

Does "fear" in either of those passages sound like "respect?" I seriously doubt the evil of impending death evokes feelings of reverence, respect or utmost regard! Neither do I usually pair up words like "high regard" or "reverence" with "dread." In these passages, good, old-fashioned fear fits the context much better.

Jesus addressed this concept of fear in the following lesson, found in two places with slightly different wording, in the New Testament.

And I say unto you my friends, Be not afraid of them that kill the body, and after that have no more that they can do. But I will forewarn you whom ye shall fear: Fear him, which after he hath killed hath power to cast into hell; yea, I say unto you, Fear him. Luke 12:4-5.

And fear not them which kill the body, but are not able to kill the soul: but rather fear him which is able to destroy both soul and body in hell. Matthew 10:28.

Everybody's afraid of something. If you were suddenly faced with the object of your very own personal fear—a hungry shark, a poisonous spider, a gun pointed at you by a very, very angry man, would you suddenly be overwhelmed by feelings of deep respect, high regard, and reverence for the object of your fear? I would think not!

Jesus was talking about God when he said "him which is able to destroy both body and soul in hell." Some people think this phrase refers to Satan, but they give the devil too much credit—Satan simply doesn't have that kind of juice. So, why did Jesus use the well-understood human fear of being *killed* as a reference point for his lesson on Godly fear, if he was not talking about the same feeling?

Taking all this in context, it would appear that God wants us to fear him, with fear as we know it. In other words,

> a. We should fear God.
> b. We should respect God.
> c. a. and b. do not mean the same thing.

Jesus' teaching on fear puts to rest any misinterpretation of God's thoughts on the topic. No matter how I look at it, there's really no way around it.

God wants me to be afraid of him.

Chapter 2

Why does God want me to be afraid of him?

Because God wants me to obey him, whether I understand his instructions or not.

To understand this, we have to look at the body's response to fear—or what fear makes you do.

If fear is sudden and extreme, it causes you to freeze or suspend all controlled activity. I specify controlled activity, because eye bulging, high-pitched babbling or cat-like mewling, uncontrollable trembling as you attempt to become the first human pretzel and other such hysterical craziness occurs quite frequently. Terror literally scares you out of your mind.

After things settle down a bit and you locate your lost mind, the first thing you do is search for a quick route of escape. If there's no hope of winning a fight, it will have to be flight, driven by that skilled get-away driver of yours, Mr. Adrenaline. But what if Mr. A can't drive you fast or far enough?

Can any hide himself in secret places that I

shall not see him? saith the LORD. Do not
I fill heaven and earth? saith the LORD.
Jeremiah 23:24.

Whither shall I go from thy spirit? or whither
shall I flee from thy presence? If I ascend up
into heaven, thou art there: if I make my bed
in hell, behold, thou art there. Psalm 139:7-8.

You're trapped! Your hope drains, as a feeling of utter powerlessness overtakes you. This is your worst nightmare. Your love of control is more than your love of life itself. The one thing you fear above all else is the loss of choice, the choice of how to live and die on your own terms. Here you are, standing powerless before the object of your fear, and there is nothing you can do about it.

So what happens if that object of fear gives you an instruction? You do a strange thing—you dare to hope again! It's a thin sliver of hope but you will grab it with both hands. Your only shot at survival is obedience, so you obey, and do so quickly. As many instructions as you are given, you carry out, quickly, and to the best of your ability. Ultimately, the person you fear is the person you will obey, without question.

Fear-based obedience is unconditional.

How is this different from the obedience that comes from deep respect, or reverence?

A person gains your respect, based on your favorable assessment of what they say and do. If they keep producing simple, effective solutions to problems for which you previously had no answers, your respect grows. You seek them out for good advice, and they become your "life guru." In other words, your respect lives and endures as long as the guru has the ability to deliver what you consider to be sound advice.

But what if the "life guru" gives you advice that you consider to be unsound? Questions abound..."Are you sure that is what you really want me to do? If you don't mind my asking, please explain...I'm confused, life guru. For real?"

If the request is particularly outlandish, I mean *really* out there, like "Take off all your clothes and walk to work naked today," or "Could you kill your son and cook him for me, please?" may I dare to suggest that your response might become a tad less diplomatic? Would it be a safe bet to assume you would not obey those instructions, as you rapidly lose respect for your "life guru?"

Respect-based obedience is conditional.

With respect or reverence, my obedience is based *on the kind of instruction I am given*. That version of obedience lacks the unshakable resolve required to carry out certain tasks, such as these:

> *Spake the LORD by Isaiah the son of Amoz,*
> *saying, Go and loose the sackcloth from off thy*

loins, and put off thy shoe from thy foot. And he did so, walking naked and barefoot. Isaiah 20:2-3.

Take now thy son, thine only son Isaac, whom thou lovest, and get thee into the land of Moriah; and offer him there for a burnt offering upon one of the mountains which I will tell thee of. And Abraham rose up early in the morning, and saddled his ass, and took two of his young men with him, and Isaac his son, and clave the wood for the burnt offering, and rose up, and went unto the place of which God had told him. Genesis 22:2-3.

So, at God's request, the prophet Isaiah went to work naked, and Abraham set out—early in the morning, no less—to turn his precious son Isaac into a meat kebab, because God had asked him to the day before! Isaiah walked to his office, naked, not for one day, but for... *three years.* Well, that's an inconvenient truth, if there ever was one! I'm confused, God. For real?

Then said I, Woe is me! for I am undone; because I am a man of unclean lips, and I dwell in the midst of a people of unclean lips: for mine eyes have seen the King, the LORD of hosts. Isaiah 6:5.

Lay not thine hand upon the lad, neither do thou any thing unto him: for now I know that <u>thou fearest God</u>, seeing thou hast not withheld thy son, thine only son from me. And Abraham lifted up his eyes. Genesis 22:12-13.

Yes, for real. Fear-based obedience has nothing to do with my understanding, agreeing with, or feeling like doing what I am being asked to do. I do it because I have to, no matter what. I fear God. This means that I obey him without question.

Fear makes me obey God, no matter the weather.

Chapter 3

Fear makes me obey God, no matter the weather. Even though we now see this to be true, it still feels weird to say it, doesn't it?

But you have just walked with me through the whole fear versus respect process. You have seen the truth. Don't worry about how it feels.

> *Trust in the LORD with all thine heart; and lean not unto thine own understanding. Proverbs 3:5.*

We can now add "Godly fear" to our God toolbox. It needs to be the very first tool in and, believe it or not, the first tool pulled out of that box. But the big question is... why?

> *Because Godly fear is the start of wisdom, and without wisdom, we <u>cannot</u> enter the kingdom of God.*

I don't know about you, but the stakes suddenly went up, way up, on this fear thing. It certainly deserves a second look, if it is that important.

In God's eyes, there are only two kinds of people—wise people, and foolish people. There are no "in between" people.

> *He that is not with me is against me: and he that gathereth not with me scattereth. Luke11:23.*

Now, I have read many Bible stories, and probably even more Bible instructions. I have noticed a very consistent pattern in them. As simplistic as this may sound, in those stories and instructions, how many consistently foolish people end up in God's kingdom? None! Wise people end up in the kingdom. Foolish ones do not.

> *Hear instruction, and be wise, and refuse it not. Blessed is the man that heareth me, watching daily at my gates, waiting at the posts of my doors. For whoso findeth me findeth life, and shall obtain favour of the LORD. Proverbs 8:33-35.*

> *Then shall the kingdom of heaven be likened unto ten virgins, which took their lamps, and went forth to meet the bridegroom. And five of them were wise, and five were foolish... they that were ready went in with him to the marriage: and the door was shut. Afterward came also the other virgins, saying, Lord,*

Lord, open to us. But he answered and said, Verily I say unto you, I know you not. Matthew 25:1-2, 10-12.

For thou art not a God that hath pleasure in wickedness: neither shall evil dwell with thee. The foolish shall not stand in thy sight. Psalm 5:4-5.

For wrath killeth the foolish man, and envy slayeth the silly one. Job 5:2.

Suddenly wisdom has jumped up several notches of importance, in my book! It has just become mission critical to become wise, as wisdom appears to be a compulsory requirement for God's favor, and his kingdom.

Now you understand why I've taken the time to develop a taste for feeling small and helpless before God. If the fear of the Lord is the beginning of wisdom, then the fear of the Lord is where the kingdom of God *starts*. We cannot enter this kingdom without it!

A kingdom is anyplace that the will of its king is done. Look at these particulars of The Lord's Prayer, the Bible's most popular prayer:

Our Father which art in heaven,
Hallowed be thy name. Thy kingdom come,
Thy will be done on earth as it is in heaven.

How many angels in God's heavenly kingdom do you think disobey God's instructions to them? Do you think heaven's angels just walk away with a "No can do God; send someone else, if you will please" attitude? I can assure you, the ones that did no longer live there!

The angels that live in heaven obey God unconditionally. We now know respect alone can't create that kind of response. Even love will not guarantee unconditional obedience. We disobey loved ones if we think, either correctly or incorrectly, that we are acting in their best interest. But angels obey the one they fear most. To be in that heavenly kingdom, so must we.

> *Behold, the kingdom of God is within you. Luke 17:21.*

If, as the scripture above says, God's kingdom comes to earth in us, the same rules of unconditional obedience that ensure his will is done must apply.

> *Wisdom is the principal thing; therefore get wisdom. Proverbs 4:7.*

I guess fear is the beginning of the principal thing. Therefore get fear and its faithful foot soldier, unconditional obedience.

But there is a whole other untapped layer to unwavering obedience that we have not yet discussed. Let's look at unconditional obedience to God from another angle, and gain a fresh, even more revealing view of it.

Think of you being in a large forest fire from which there appears to be no escape. Suddenly somebody comes running up to you with a precise map of the only specific pathway out of that forest. He tells you to follow him and do exactly what he says and does, if you want to live.

If you don't believe him and refuse to follow him, you will die. If you agree to follow him but don't pay attention to his instructions, either because you are paralyzed by fear of the fiery forest, or cocky overconfidence, you will still die.

But if you begin to think it is possible to get out alive, and you are more afraid of this individual than the paralyzing fear you may have of the fiery forest, you will obey what he says without question and live.

So, I guess it all comes down to this…I understand that I am in trouble (forest fire). I am met by a man who tells me there is a way out (possible savior?) but I must do exactly what he says to live.

If I choose to believe and fear him, I obey him and live (unconditional obedience, salvation…he *is* my savior! I love this guy!) If I choose not to, I sit in the forest fire and die (death).

Note the order of events very carefully. Your savior is not your savior until you actually do what he says. You must make him the "lord" of your forest fire escape route. Your continued unwavering obedience to him *all the way to your exit from the forest* is how you get saved from the forest fire.

Lordship <u>always</u> comes first, before salvation.

In other words, you must take on the role of a servant to be saved. And since fear is what creates unwavering obedience, fear of your lord must be present at all times to ensure and complete your salvation.

> *Wherefore, my beloved, as ye have <u>always</u> <u>obeyed</u>, not as in my presence only, but now much more in my absence, <u>work out your own</u> <u>salvation</u> with fear and trembling. Philippians 2:12.*

What is the relationship of a lord to his servant? The lord, in just about every way protects and provides for his servant. The lord feeds, houses, clothes and provides all necessities for his servant. If anyone is insolent to or hurts the servant, that person has disrespected the lord and will feel the wrath of the lord, before all is said and done.

The responsibility of a servant to his lord is much simpler. The servant does what his lord asks him to do, without question.

Unconditional obedience is the only compulsory requirement of a servant towards his lord. You should respect your lord. If he is a good lord, you will grow to love your lord—as you get to know him. But from the get go, and at all times during your employment with him, you must do what he says without question. Those are the terms of your employment.

So, I guess the big fuss about fear and unconditional obedience is that they are necessary for you to have a lord, and having a lord is necessary for you to be saved.

You are going to need both fear and its special brand of obedience if you are going to have Jesus Christ as your Lord. Only after you have chosen <u>and</u> obeyed him as Lord can Jesus be your Savior, or "Christ."

> *Unconditional obedience is a really big deal,*
> *if you are going to have Jesus of Nazareth as*
> *your Lord, and Christ.*

Chapter 4

I choose Jesus of Nazareth as my Lord! When I obey him unconditionally, he becomes my Christ! This correct sequence of events is of the utmost importance, which is why the Bible writes them...*in sequence.*

> *If thou shalt confess with thy mouth the <u>Lord Jesus</u>, and shalt believe in thine heart that God hath raised him from the dead, thou shalt be <u>saved</u>. For with the heart man believeth unto righteousness; and with the mouth confession is made unto salvation. Romans 10:9-10.*

> *Therefore let all the house of Israel know assuredly, that God hath made that same Jesus, whom ye have crucified, both <u>Lord</u> and <u>Christ</u>. Acts 2:36.*

Did you catch it? Lord and all that it entails comes first and then, Christ. Christ comes from the Greek word Christos which means "Savior," or "Messiah." Switching the sequence does not come up with the same result—try baking a cake with the sequence of instructions backwards!

Now that is a huge deal; suddenly, it redefines what it means to be Christian. Christian means Christ follower. The reason for "ineffective Christianity" today is a loss of this correct sequence.

The many versions of the sinner's prayer I have heard emphasize getting saved over accepting lordship— they bake the cake backwards! I believe this is the most misunderstood part of the Bible today. The "new convert" is so excited at being saved, he totally forgets about lordship. Meaning, in effect, he does not obey God's instructions, and is by definition, not Christian at all. Listen to the sobering words from the Lord Jesus himself:

> *Not every one that saith unto me, Lord, Lord, shall enter into the kingdom of heaven; but he that doeth the will of my Father which is in heaven. Matthew 7:21.*

> *And why call ye me, Lord, Lord, and do not the things which I say? Luke 6:46.*

But as we have seen fear and lordship are linked together. You really cannot have one without the other. Jesus wants me to fear him; otherwise it is impossible to be saved by him. Yes, you did not mishear what I just said.

Kiss the Son, lest he be angry, and ye perish from the way, when his wrath is kindled but a little. Psalm 2:12.

Which "Son" do you think King David was talking about? Jesus Christ, the Son of God, of course!

His Lordship is what assures your salvation, and not the other way round. He is my forest fire savior. But I must first hope he can be my savior, choose to believe, act on this hope and fear him more than the forest fire, to make heaven.

For we are saved by hope. Romans 8:24.

What is so interesting is that there are already familiar models that show the heavenly application of this fear in our world today. God uses the physical world to demonstrate the ways things work in the spiritual one. Productive fear has lived around you unrecognized for a long time, in ways that you have accepted without casting it as some sort of villain.

Verily, verily, I say unto thee, Except a man be born again, he cannot see the kingdom of God. John 3:3.

Every labor and delivery ward has a special sound that we know very well. It warms our hearts with the wonder of life's new beginning. It is the symphony of a baby's cry as it is born. But why do they cry?

Some say it is to rid the lungs of fluid or water and open them up for proper breathing. But we all know the process necessary for such activity is called vigorous coughing. The cough reflex is developed while the child is still in the womb during pregnancy, so that can't be the reason for crying.

Others have said the reason for crying at birth is hunger. But children do not have crying faces during baby ultrasound pictures, and the child is still attached to the mother by an umbilical cord, at birth. Therefore crying should start only after the cord is cut. No, hunger isn't the issue.

I have also heard it said that babies feel cold immediately after birth, hence the crying. But this cannot be true either. If it was, babies born in hot climates would not cry. The temperature of the average human body is about 98.6F. It is not at all uncommon to have that as the environment's temperature, at various times and places in the world. Babies born at such times and in such places should not cry at birth, but they do.

> *New-borne babies cry because they are afraid.*

Here's another example. You have just changed jobs. What is the feeling you have towards your new boss on day one at the job, the day you are practically falling over yourself to do your new boss's every bidding?

Is what you feel toward your new boss respect? Not really. You just met the new boss. There hasn't been enough time for you to develop that emotion. Love, maybe? Well, love at first sight is possible, but that's certainly not the way to start out your new work career. As we had discussed earlier, with love, you might make a well-meaning mistake and hear those dreadful three words you are afraid to hear—"You are fired!"

Did I just hear what I thought I heard; you thinking about that much castigated word, "afraid?" I do believe you just did! Because fear is exactly what you feel towards your new boss on day one of your new job.

> *Servants, be obedient to them that are your masters according to the flesh, with fear and trembling, in singleness of your heart, as unto Christ. Ephesians 6:5.*

> *Servants, be subject to your masters with all fear; not only to the good and gentle, but also to the froward. 1 Peter 2:18.*

You may grow to respect the new boss after a while, even love the new boss later as you catch their vision, but what you feel at first is fear of the new boss, or "master." Fear that makes you nervously perform all the tasks required of you that day, because the boss has the power to fire you and to taint your work history forever, and you would be powerless to stop it. So, you knuckle under, and do as you are told.

> *You are afraid of your new boss.*

As well you should be. Or you might have a serious problem putting food on the table, for both you and your family. Then where would you be?

We could go on with other examples of productive fear—the fear of falling from a great height, of getting burned by fire, the fear of suffocation, or a child's fear of punishment—in whatever form it may take—"when Daddy gets home," to name a few. They, along with our two examples above share one thing in common; you are helpless in the face of what you fear.

> *Ye shall fear every man his mother, and his father. Leviticus 19:3.*

> *Render therefore to all their dues: tribute to whom tribute is due; custom to whom custom; fear to whom fear; honour to whom honour. Romans 13:7.*

It is also not necessarily the intent of the feared one to cause us grievous bodily harm. In fact in the two explained examples, the feared one actually wants us to do well—the boss doesn't want to go through the process of hiring yet another rookie, and the smiling parent leans forward to whisper in the crying little baby's ear:

> Hush little baby, don't you cry,
> I'm gonna love you till the day I die…

Or until the day you turn thirteen, whichever comes first. All jokes aside, Jesus' use of the phrase "born again" was not by accident. Spiritual birth and physical birth are connected.

> *Verily, verily, I say unto thee, Except a man be born of <u>water</u> and of <u>the Spirit</u>, he cannot enter into the kingdom of God. That which is born of the flesh is flesh; and that which is born of the Spirit is spirit. Marvel not: that I said unto thee, Ye must be born again. John 3:5-7.*

> *Verily I say unto you, Whosoever shall not receive the kingdom of God as a little child shall in no wise enter therein. Luke 18:17.*

Jesus used these analogies because physical birth has uncanny similarities to spiritual birth. The former is a symbol of the latter, and we learn about one by looking at the other. Both babies express fear at birth. A baby that doesn't cry after its birth is a source of urgency and panic for those of us in the world of the living.

> *A baby, be it physical or spiritual, that does not experience fear after its birth is dead.*

Chapter 5

So, what shall we do?

This is my favorite question in the entire Bible. This is the question that comes from people who are ready to change course, but don't quite know how.

> *Now when they heard this, they were pricked in their heart, and said unto Peter and to the rest of the apostles, Men and brethren, what shall we do? Acts 2:37.*

> *And the soldiers likewise demanded of him, saying, And what shall we do? Luke 3:14.*

> *Then came also publicans to be baptized, and said unto him, Master, what shall we do? Luke 3:12.*

> *And he trembling and astonished said, Lord, what wilt thou have me to do? Acts 9:6.*

Now you are ready to be instructed. Until that point, you are a know-it-all—either a skeptic, arrogant, or judgmental. God cannot get through the walls you have erected until you allow yourself to ask the "what shall I do" question. Only then can the Holy Spirit go to work.

So what shall we do?

1. Learn how to be afraid of God.

Think about those examples of those fears we gave earlier in the book, of " them that kill the body"—an angry person with a knife to your throat or a thief with a gun to your head, an enraged herd of bulls charging straight at you, a poisonous spider or snake bite, a hungry shark—take your pick.

Now take that fear you have and transfer it. Transfer it to God, the only one who can destroy both your body and soul. How does this work, in practical terms?

I know this thing I want to do is bad. But I really, *really* want to do it. If I knew the consequence was of a hungry shark *slowly* munching off my leg—in my mind's eye, I can actually see the shark poised to bite—would I still do it? If the answer is no, then I will not do it. It is unacceptable for me to fear a hungry shark more than I fear God.

> *And I say unto you my friends, Be not afraid of them that kill the body, and after that have no more that they can do. But I will forewarn you whom ye shall fear: Fear him, which after he hath killed hath power to cast into hell; yea, I say unto you, Fear him. Luke 12:4-5.*

> *And fear not them which kill the body, but*
> *are not able to kill the soul: but rather fear*
> *him which is able to destroy both soul and*
> *body in hell. Matthew 10:28.*

Maybe your fear flavor is more about humans with guns to your head, as you have mastered the art of kicking hungry sharks in the nose. If I was told that I would be shot in the head if I performed the action, would I still do it? If I wouldn't touch that action with a ten foot pole, then I choose to not perform the action. It is unacceptable for me to obey a gunman more than I obey God.

> *Then Peter and the other apostles answered*
> *and said, We ought to obey God rather than*
> *men. Acts 5:29.*

> *And they called them, and commanded them*
> *not to speak at all nor teach in the name of*
> *Jesus. But Peter and John answered and said*
> *unto them, Whether it be right in the sight*
> *of God to hearken unto you more than unto*
> *God, judge ye. Acts 4:18-19.*

I think you get the picture now. This somewhat gruesome, but effective training regimen trains you on Godly fear. Whenever I have a decision to make, I must pull out the fear of the Lord first, and hold up my decision to the discerning eye of this fear. Does my decision clash with my fear of God? If it does, my decision has to go. I must discard it and make another decision.

But some people ask, "How do I know if the action is right or wrong? I just want God to tell me what to do!" What to do in such cases? Here's a simple decision tool that should do the trick.

If God was standing three feet from me, would I feel comfortable doing this activity? If the answer is no, then the action is wrong. If the answer is yes, go right ahead and do the activity. If your action is wrong you will not be held accountable for it, though God will probably let you know in due course that you made an incorrect decision. This is the attitude of someone who is *pure in heart*. You need to truthfully evaluate your actions at all times.

2. Be true to yourself, with no guile.

Be totally honest with yourself. No guile! Satan told the first lie—to himself. Lies started all creation's troubles and only the truth can fix them. The habitually truthful person is "pure in heart," whether his decisions are right or wrong. These are the people that God calls into his presence and partners with, to do his work.

> *Blessed are the pure in heart: for they shall see God. Matthew 5:8.*

> *Jesus saw Nathanael coming to him, and saith of him, Behold an Israelite indeed, in whom is no guile! John 1:47.*

*Who shall ascend into the hill of the LORD?
or who shall stand in his holy place? He that
hath clean hands, and a pure heart. Psalm
24:3-4.*

We have just learned how to obey God with fear
and integrity. How do we put these two together in
practice? There is a simple technique that contains both
these elements. Think like a soldier.

3. Trust and obey your commanding officer.

A soldier understands unconditional obedience.
He is aware that his commanding officer is his "lord"
or master on the battlefield. He fears his commanding
officer and understands that his carrying out his job
ensures the safety of his comrades. The field mission is
bigger than his needs or wants.

A soldier understands honesty, because where
there is integrity, there is trust. He must trust his
commanding officer and do what the commander
says, just as much as his commander must trust him
to carry out those orders. The moment he distrusts his
commanding officer is the moment he is liable for a
court-martial, because he will disobey direct orders or
he will desert his post, costing precious lives.

The Bible tells us who we are through God's eyes.
God tells us in the Bible that we are his *soldiers.*

*Wherefore take unto you the whole armour
of God, that ye may be able to withstand in*

> *the evil day, and having done all, to stand.*
> *Ephesians 6:13.*

> *But let us, who are of the day, be sober, put-*
> *ting on the breastplate of faith and love; and*
> *for an helmet, the hope of salvation. 1 Thes-*
> *salonians 5:8.*

> *For the weapons of our warfare are not*
> *carnal, but mighty through God to the*
> *pulling down of strong holds. 2 Corinthians*
> *10:4.*

A soldier's mentality stops us from becoming victims of circumstance and instead makes us initiators of events. We are in a war not of our own choosing but we are in one, nonetheless. Our survival depends on our thinking like a people at war.

Therefore, making myself nothing by fearing God and obeying him wins my war. Establishing my own identity, my own point of view and adding snippets of God's instructions to my own personally approved list of instructions doesn't get the job done. This latter approach, the one mostly in play in our world today, comes from a place of pride and rebellion. It does not meet the standard for entry into God's kingdom.

Well my friends, I have given you all I know on the fear of the Lord, its connection to obeying God's word and wisdom. This ends the first section. I'll leave you with these Bible quotes to underline the need to

live your life wisely. We will discuss the word and the
wisdom of God in the next section.

> *Therefore whosoever heareth these sayings of
> mine, and doeth them, I will liken him unto
> a wise man, which built his house upon a
> rock: And the rain descended, and the floods
> came, and the winds blew, and beat upon
> that house; and it fell not: for it was founded
> upon a rock. Matthew 7:24-25.*

> *And every one that heareth these sayings of
> mine, and doeth them not, shall be likened
> unto a foolish man, which built his house
> upon the sand: And the rain descended, and
> the floods came, and the winds blew, and
> beat upon that house; and it fell: and great
> was the fall of it. Matthew 7:26-27.*

THE WORD & THE WISDOM OF GOD

Christ the power of God,
and the wisdom of God.
1 Corinthians 1:24.

Chapter 6

What is the Word of God?

Well, it is exactly as it sounds. The Word of God is God's words, spoken, written or symbolized. All the words God ever spoke put together.

Here, "Word" is used in its singular form as a summary of all God's words. It is used in the same way we cheer and shout "Word!" indicating all the words of an eloquent speaker, just after they have delivered a powerful speech. But what do words actually do?

Words are instructions, or commands.

For example, I want to catch the attention of a man called "Gillis" from across a room full of people. I could shout out "Gillis!" If he hears, he will turn and pay attention to me.

I could write "Gillis" on a piece of paper and have it hand-delivered across the room. Gillis will read the note and look around enquiringly for who wrote it. He has been instructed that somebody wants his attention. Or I could wave my hands repeatedly and insistently at "Gillis," until I catch his attention. He will look over inquisitively at me. Once again, I have caught his attention.

Now let's explore a slightly different scenario. Gillis has just bumped his head and passed out, unconscious on the floor. Would Gillis respond, if I waved at him, shouted his name, or passed him a note with his name on it? No, he would not. For the moment, Gillis is blind, deaf, and paralyzed.

We have just learned something very interesting about words. They are instructions that create results *only when they are perceived, and acted upon.* For the Word of God to fulfill its capacity to create amazing results, it must first be perceived, and then acted upon.

Let's learn some other characteristics of God's Word.

> *In the beginning God created the heaven and the earth. Genesis 1:1.*

> *In the beginning was the Word, and the Word was with God, and the Word was God. The same was in the beginning with God. <u>All things were made by him</u>; and without him was not any thing made that was made. John 1:1-3.*

> *God, who at sundry times and in divers manners spake in time past unto the fathers by the prophets, Hath in these last days spoken unto us by his Son, whom he hath appointed heir of all things, <u>by whom also he made the worlds</u>. Hebrews 1:1-2.*

These three statements tell us a lot about the Word of God.

The Word of God created everything. God kept speaking instruction after instruction or "word," and creation kept appearing until everything was created.

The Word of God is male. The statements keep referring to the Word as "he." If the Word created everything, then the Word, for his own reasons, designated himself as "he." There are females also in creation. They are called "she."

The Word of God is contained inside the Son of God. The Word of God has to be inside God's Son, since the passages above describe the Son and the Word as having done the exact same thing—"create the worlds," both earthly and heavenly.

The Word of God continues to give us instructions today. The Hebrews passage above says God's instructions speak to us through his Son, in "these last days," meaning now. Therefore the Word did not only give instructions that created everything in the beginning, but gives those same creation instructions to us today, as a manual of how all created things work.

Lastly, *the Word of God is the power of God.* What is power? Power is the ability to act or produce an effect—Merriam-Webster online dictionary.

The Word of God created an effect all right; all that is in our world, and beyond! Did you hear the passage above, from the book of John? Without the Word of God "was not anything made that was made." Therefore, God's power is in the Word that he speaks.

Where the word of a king is, there is power.
Ecclesiastes 8:4.

To recap, the Word of God is all of God's instructions ever spoken, put together. God's Word at the beginning of time created the whole universe, and continues to instruct us on how it works, to this very day. God's power resides in his Word, but this power can only be unleashed and yield results if God's instructions are understood and acted upon. The entire Word of God dwells in God's Son. And God's Word is a male.

Chapter 7

Wisdom's a woman.

Don't scoff, men. Your wives have been right all along. I guess that includes mine too. At least that's what the Bible has to say on the matter.

> *Say unto wisdom, Thou art my sister; and call understanding thy kinswoman. Proverbs 7:4.*

This is not a one-time female representation of wisdom either. Whenever the Bible talks about wisdom as person, wisdom is female. Every single time.

> *Wisdom crieth without; she uttereth her voice in the streets: She crieth in the chief place of concourse, in the openings of the gates. Proverbs 1:20-21.*
>
> *Wisdom hath builded her house, she hath hewn out her seven pillars. Proverbs 9:1.*
>
> *But wisdom is justified of all her children. Luke 7:35.*

Of course, the Holy Scripture does not always represent wisdom as a person. Much like "Word," "wisdom" is also used in ways that are much more familiar to our secular understanding of the term. But what exactly does wisdom do?

Wisdom explains and applies good instructions.

Wisdom: The ability or result of an ability to think and act utilizing knowledge, experience, understanding, common sense, and insight—Collins English Dictionary.

For example, I offer you a taste of an exotic fruit that you have never eaten before. I have eaten it and know how delicious it is. So I encourage you to trust me, urge you to taste the fruit, you do so and...Yum! The next time you run into that fruit, you know what it tastes like. You will pick it up and eat it, no questions asked. You have acquired wisdom regarding the exotic fruit.

O taste and see that the LORD is good:
blessed is the man that trusteth in him.
Psalm 34:8.

How sweet are thy words unto my taste!
Psalm 119:103.

Here's another example. You've been standing for

a long period of time, trying (and failing) to complete an important task. I can tell your legs are tired, and your concentration is shot. So I pull up an empty chair behind you and invite you to sit down in it. You sit and suddenly, Bliss! Your concentration returns and you finish the task. You have just gained wisdom on how to best perform that important task—it is best done sitting down!

> *And Moses said unto Joshua, Choose us out men, and go out, fight with Amalek: to morrow I will stand on the top of the hill with the rod of God in mine hand...But Moses' hands were heavy; and they took a stone, and put it under him, and he sat thereon. Exodus 17:9-12.*

Did you notice that you first have to follow instructions to get wisdom? Put another way, the "Word" or command is *obeyed first*; then you get the wisdom! This is the same for both the familiar—"sit down in a chair," and the unfamiliar—"eat an exotic fruit." In God's economy, it really makes no difference. Obey first; you'll enjoy me later. The wisdom always existed in the action, but you cannot obtain that wisdom until you do what you are told.

So, "Word" is *what* I do, "wisdom" is *why* and *how* I do it, and I must do word to get wisdom. Let's learn a few more things about wisdom.

The LORD by wisdom <u>hath founded the earth</u>; by understanding hath he <u>established the heavens</u>. Proverbs 3:19.

Doth not wisdom cry? and understanding put forth her voice? She standeth in the top of high places, by the way in the places of the paths. She crieth at the gates, at the entry of the city, at the coming in at the doors. Unto you, O men, I call; and my voice is to the sons of man. Proverbs 8:1-4.

The LORD possessed me in the beginning of his way, before his works of old...I was daily his delight, rejoicing always before him. Proverbs 8:22, 30.

Happy is the man that findeth wisdom, and the man that getteth understanding... She is more precious than rubies: and all the things thou canst desire are not to be compared unto her...Her ways are ways of pleasantness, and all her paths are peace. Proverbs 3:13, 15, 17.

These four passages tell us several important things about wisdom.

Wisdom and the Word created everything. Wisdom founded the heavens and the earth. This makes the Word and wisdom partners in the creation of all things.

Wisdom is contained inside the Son of God. Wisdom in its entirety must be contained in the Son of God in much the same way as the Word is, since we know from the previous chapter that all things were made by the Son of God.

Wisdom is enjoyed by God. We see wisdom described above as being a source of delight to God. This evokes a vivid image of wisdom and God, thoroughly enjoying each other's company.

Wisdom enjoys people. Wisdom stands calling out to people, in all the places where people are found. This tells us something amazing; wisdom not only enjoys people, but she is very easy to find! Therefore, anybody who says wisdom is hard to find has chosen to ignore her constant call. She's been around you all the time!

Wisdom is enjoyed by people. For those who listen to wisdom's call, they are in for a treat—she is the most satisfying companion a person could ever have! I've heard it said diamonds are a girl's best friend, but they can't hold a candle to wisdom. And one of her most remarkable characteristics is that she brings you that rare commodity we all secretly long for...*peace.*

So wisdom is very practical, very "sweet," and thoroughly enjoyed by the people who have it. Word is male and wisdom is female, Word comes first and wisdom second, and both Word and wisdom created everything. Interesting, but what does all that have to do with me? You'll find out, in the next chapter.

Chapter 8

Why did God make man and woman?

If you haven't wondered, I certainly have. God made what would appear to be the perfect man—Adam with both female and male parts in him. An Adam in touch with his feminine side, just the way most ladies I know would like it.

Then God did a strange thing. He actually said the perfect man was "not good!" in the man-woman form that he was, took this perfect man and split him in two! Why? The man was perfect!

The "Man" (Adam Part One) called his missing body parts "Woman," which really means Adam Part Two. So, now there's more variety and diversity in the world—I get that.

> *And Adam said, This is now bone of my bones, and flesh of my flesh: she shall be called Woman, because she was taken out of Man. Genesis 2:23.*

But then God decrees the two "Adam parts" come back together, and become one again!

> *Therefore shall a man leave his father and his mother, and shall cleave unto his wife: and they shall be <u>one flesh</u>. Genesis 2:24.*

What is going on? Is this just a case of God the Father amusing himself with jigsaw puzzles? I don't think so. God revealed something by splitting Adam in two, and then putting his pieces back together again. God does nothing randomly. The secret is in the splitting; actually, the two previous chapters revealed what the secret is.

Word's a man. Wisdom's a woman.

Men represent the Word. They come first, like executive instructions. Men, like new instructions, are hard, full of uncomfortable angles which poke into you, making them unpleasant to handle or lean up against, but they provide the strong frame to carry you through trying times. If life was a tree, men are its *roots and branches.*

Women represent wisdom. Like wisdom, they come second. They have gentle hollows and soft curves, possessing a sweetness which makes them a delight to the senses and comfortable to the touch—like wisdom. If life was a tree, women are its *fruits.*

How many fruits do you know have sharp angular shapes? How many branches are smoothly curved, with pleasing hollows? How many people are attracted to a tree because of its angular roots or knobby branches? By comparison, how many people are attracted to a tree's fruits? And yet, without roots and branches growing first, no fruits will show up later, during harvest season.

God made the visible world and the things in it as symbols of the invisible world. God created both visible and invisible worlds. In the visible world, Adam and all his descendants are symbols of God himself. So men are hard, angular and unyielding, while women are softer, curvier, and generally less formidable in physical appearance.

> *For the invisible things of him from the creation of the world are clearly seen, being understood by the things that are made, even his eternal power and Godhead; so that they are without excuse. Romans 1:20.*

> *So God created man in his own image, in the image of God created he him; male and female created he them. Genesis 1:27.*

Differences in temperament are also seen. Men tend to be happier with clear-cut, performance-based tasks—pick this up, destroy this, build that...in other words, *instructions*. Women tend to be more interested in understanding feelings and how things work...*wisdom*. This difference shows up in our organizational church structure today, since church sermons focus more on teaching and are less task-oriented. There are significantly more women who willingly attend church than men.

The first man went out and faced the world first—like word. The woman stayed behind the man—like wisdom. Joined together, they were able to be fruitful, multiply, fill and dominate the earth. The first man and woman worked together in a way that was supposed to be a visible lesson of how the Word and the wisdom of God worked together in the spiritual world, being fruitful, multiplying and ruling all things created.

> *And God blessed them, and God said unto them, Be fruitful, and multiply, and replenish the earth, and subdue it. Genesis 1:28.*

Believe it or not, this is the reason that God made men and women. However, God put a time limit on this kind of activity. There would be no need for men and women to collaborate in this manner when time is finally over. The lesson would already have been learned. Therefore there will be no need for marriage then.

> *And Jesus answering said unto them, Do ye not therefore err, because ye know not the scriptures, neither the power of God? For when they shall rise from the dead, they neither marry, nor are given in marriage; but are as the angels which are in heaven. Mark 12:24-25.*

But time is not done yet. Word and wisdom if both learned at the same time would create confusion as to which one of these two wonderful entities comes first, in God's way of doing things.

Think about the exotic fruit example from the previous chapter. Once you have gained wisdom of its delicious taste and you eat it again, you obey the word with full understanding or wisdom of what you are going to experience. Or if you are standing and sit down in a chair, you sit down knowing what the chair will do for you. In other words, if you have both word and wisdom, it is hard to know which comes first, because you experience word and wisdom at the same time.

So God has made it so that in time, Word goes before wisdom, and his way is shown clearly in the earth. Time creates the space for learning God's way. But what exactly is this way that God is so insistent we learn? We will learn what it is in the next chapter.

Chapter 9

God insists on a particular characteristic for all humans. He insists that we must have *faith* to have favor. Faith is God's way. God literally says it is impossible to please him without it!

> But without faith it is impossible to please him: for he that cometh to God <u>must</u> believe that he is. Hebrews 11:6.

Whenever God puts a "must" next to something, I develop really big ears and listen. So, what does faith do? Put very simply,

> *Faith puts Word first before wisdom.*

> Faith: Strong or unshakeable belief in something, especially without proof or evidence—Collins English Dictionary.

Faith makes you act on what you believe, even if you do not understand how your action works.

We all have some faith. I do not know all the inner workings of a car, but I have faith that when I put my car keys in the ignition and start it up that the car will start and take me where I need to go. If it doesn't start up on the first turn of the ignition, I don't just walk away from the car, throw my hands up and exclaim "That's it! The car won't start!" do I? I turn the key *again*.

Looking at the example above, we can see that faith obeys instructions based on hope, with no assurance that the instructions will work, but believing they will. Also, we can see that faith has to have action attached to it for it to be really different from belief. The Bible does a much better job than Collins English Dictionary defining the action component of faith.

> *Faith is the <u>substance</u> of things hoped for, the <u>evidence</u> of things unseen Hebrews 11:1.*

> *Even so faith, if it hath not works, <u>is dead</u>, being alone. Yea, a man may say, Thou hast faith, and I have works: shew me thy faith without thy works, and I will shew thee my faith by my works. James 2:17-18.*

> *We having the same spirit of faith, according as it is written, I believed, and therefore have I spoken; we also believe, and therefore speak. 2 Corinthians 4:13.*

Therefore, my faith obeys instructions based on *trust*, whether I understand how the instructions work or not. I choose to believe in a good outcome. God's way is the way of faith, and he expects it from all people. Through faith, God created everything that exists.

> *Through faith we understand that the worlds were framed by the word of God, so that things which are seen were not made of things which do appear. Hebrews 11:3.*

Let us look at a very different way of doing things. We will investigate the way of logic. What is logic, and what does logic do?

> *Logic is acting based on a set of understood principles.*

> Logic: The system or principles of reasoning applicable to any branch of knowledge or study—Dictionary.com.

Unlike faith, logic only obeys instructions it understands. Therefore, *logic does not create anything new*. It only explains what has already been created. Faith trusts the giver of instructions. Logic trusts the receiver understanding how those instructions work— "I will only do what I understand to be good." In other words,

> *Logic puts wisdom first before Word.*

Unfortunately, my understanding is a moving

target, and so is yours. Remember the kids you thought were the coolest kids on the block in high school? Fast forward five years, to college. Are they still as cool? Zip forward another fifteen years. I don't know about you, but it would have been a *big* mistake if I had married my high school crush. Wow! My understanding changed a lot in twenty years! So did my logic.

Is logic a subset of faith? No, logic is not a part of faith, even though faith and logic will sometimes use the same methods, and produce the same results. It all boils down to why you perform an action. Do you act because you trust the instructor, or because you understand the process and the result of the instruction? The former is faith, the latter, logic.

So, which one is the correct way of doing things? Faith in God, of course! Faith creates new things, which logic cannot do. My understanding changes all the time, and therefore so does my logic—like the logic of a baby climbing unto an open fire, because the flames are "so pretty!" My faith has no such dangerous limitation, because the Word of God does not change.

> *There is a way which seemeth right unto a man, but the end thereof are the ways of death. Proverbs 14:12.*

> *The word of the Lord endureth for ever. And this is the word which by the gospel is preached unto you. 1 Peter 1:25.*

But logic, not faith is the method we are taught as the standard way of reasoning today.

Why has this method caught on like wildfire? Because of *wisdom*. Wisdom is a delight, remember? Everybody wants it, and logic seems like a shortcut to it! But, you cannot remove the roots and branches of a tree and expect its fruits to grow. You cannot remove instructions and get the prize of wisdom. It really is that simple. Just as it is proper to get the approval of a man to ask a favor of his wife,

> *You have to go through Word, to get to wisdom. There are no shortcuts.*

Chapter 10

We have now learned that man physically represents Word, and woman is a symbol for wisdom. Faith is God's way of creating life in the heavens and the earth, and involves first obeying the Word, to obtain wisdom.

Jesus of Nazareth, the Son of God, has all Word and wisdom residing in the part of him called his *spirit*. I have written about the spirit, soul and body in much more detail in my previous book *Kingdom Come: A Book of Threes*, so here we will just briefly summarize these three components of the human body, and what they do.

Every human being has a spirit, a soul and a fleshly body. The spirit's boss should be God, the soul's boss should be the spirit and the body's boss—well, everybody is his boss, but his immediate boss should be the soul.

The *spirit* is the container of all instructions for the individual. These instructions start in the womb from the moment of conception. The spirit instructs the fertilized egg to divide into two cells, to multiply and to differentiate into different body parts, long before you even have a brain. It is filled with good instructions placed in it by God, and/or bad instructions placed in it by Satan.

The *soul* is the choice maker of the person. It is the working output of a person's brain, unlike the spirit, which is full of instructions that each have a specific effect. The soul is shaped through learning, emotions and decisions about which words to obey and which ones to ignore. The soul actually decides what words are allowed into its boss, the spirit, unless it decides to give up that choice! A person's choices over time determine personality, or character.

The *body* is that tangible flesh pouch that carries the spirit and soul around. It shows the outcome of what the soul decides. The body is best when the soul chooses to obey good instructions, and worst when the soul chooses bad instructions, given it by the spirit. You want to see the handiwork of a spirit and the choices of its soul, whether they are good or bad? Look at the body.

There is an old story said to have been written by the prophet Ezekiel, about a king whose palace was robbed. The king was very upset and came out on the palace steps where two beggars, one blind and the other lame were sitting. The king asked the blind beggar if he had seen the thief.

"My king, how could I have seen the thief, seeing that I am blind?" replied the blind beggar.

The king turned to the lame beggar and asked him if he had seen the thief.

"O my king, how could I have seen anything since I cannot walk and he must have escaped from some other part of your palace?"

The king thought a minute. Then he walked up to the lame beggar, picked him up and put him, piggyback style, on the back of the blind beggar.

"That is how both of you stole my treasure from my palace."

Such is the relationship between body, soul and, in this case, a stealing spirit. Needless to say, it did not end well for either soul or body.

Now, getting back to Jesus' spirit,

> And the Word was made flesh, and dwelt among us, (and we beheld his glory, the glory as of the only begotten of the Father,) full of grace and truth...For the law was given by Moses, but grace and truth came by Jesus Christ. John 1:14-17.

> But unto them which are called, both Jews and Greeks, Christ the power of God, and the wisdom of God. 1 Corinthians 1:24.

> He hath made the earth by his power, he hath established the world by his wisdom, and hath stretched out the heaven by his understanding. Jeremiah 51:15.

Both male and female components fully reside in the spirit of Jesus Christ, even though he is a man. Adam the first man was exactly the same way, but he was split to teach him over time what makes life work—

faith, which puts Word before wisdom, which in turn creates fruitfulness and multiplication.

Unfortunately, "the Adams" gave in to Satan's temptation and chose wisdom first over Word—the first recorded instance of logical behavior. Satan knew exactly what eating the fruit would do, because he knew the Garden of Eden, and all its fruits.

> *Thus saith the Lord GOD; Thou sealest up the sum, full of wisdom, and perfect in beauty. Thou hast been in Eden the garden of God. Ezekiel 28:12-13.*

> *When the woman saw that the tree was good for food, and that it was pleasant to the eyes, and a tree to be desired <u>to make one wise</u>, she took of the fruit thereof, and did eat. Genesis 3:6.*

How did Satan know what would happen? Because, as the passage above tells us, he was the sum of wisdom before he fell. He had once stood over the mercy seat in God's throne room as a covering cherub, witnessing most of the creation process! But his weakness is revealed by his very nature. What is missing from his makeup? He may have had wisdom, but he never contained *Word*.

Satan cannot speak things into being!

Only God and humans can do that. Satan insisted he wanted Word to go along with his wisdom, fought God for it and fell, losing his wisdom. But Satan still has knowledge of what he saw when he was in God's throne room. It is no mistake that Satan tempted the woman. He knew exactly whom she represented, and what had been taken from him.

> *How art thou fallen from heaven, O Lucifer, son of the morning! how art thou cut down to the ground, which didst weaken the nations! For thou hast said in thine heart...I will be like the most High. Isaiah 14:12-14.*

So, Satan belongs to a league of fallen cherubim, men and women were made as earthly symbols, and Adam initially had a feminine side—this is all quite interesting, but what does all this mean, for us?

a. Be <u>very, very</u> careful with your words.

People, like God, have power by the words we speak. We create good or evil with them. Satan's area of attack is by influencing humans to speak evil into earthly being, since he really cannot do this himself. It is our job to resist any urge to use bad words, or verbally condone acts of evil.

> *Death and life are in the power of the tongue. Proverbs 18:21.*

Bless we God, even the Father; and therewith curse we men, which are made after the similitude of God. Out of the same mouth proceedeth blessing and cursing. My brethren, these things ought not so to be. James 3:9-10.

b. *Choose faith over logic.*

Become expert at following God's instructions to the T. The fear of the Lord achieves this. This takes training, but God is a God of grace, a characteristic that we will discuss in more detail later. The correct sequence is to obey God's instructions first. Your obedience brings you wisdom.

Hear counsel, and receive instruction, that thou mayest be wise in thy <u>latter end</u>. Proverbs 19:20.

c. *Jesus Christ made all life.*

Jesus is the only human being that contains life's total blueprint. Therefore he is the only way given unto men and women to live as was intended.

And Jesus answered him, saying, It is written, That man shall not live by bread alone, but by every word of God. Luke 4:4.

Jesus saith unto him, I am the way, the truth, and the life: no man cometh unto the Father, but by me. John 14:6.

For there is none other name under heaven given among men, whereby we must be saved. Acts 4:12.

There is no other way to live but through what Jesus, the Word of God, tells us to do, and Jesus, the wisdom of God, makes us understand and apply. Only then have we truly manifested God the Father's glory as was intended, and become God's children.

This ends the Word and wisdom section. Summarizing it all in a couple of sentences is easy.

Obey the Word of God to get his wisdom. This is the way of faith, and life.

THE PEACE OF GOD

*Peace I leave with you, my peace I give unto
you: not as the world giveth.
John 14:27.*

Chapter 11

Everyone's looking for peace.
It is amazing how universally true this is. People
may try different ways to get it, but peace is a
garment that's always in fashion.

Maybe we crave peace so much because it is closely
linked to rest, and we are made for both. Peaceful is the
soul that rests. After all, most of us recognize the need
for rest, and we have a compulsory dose of it when we
sleep. Even the most dedicated workaholics have to
sleep sometime.

But Jesus of Nazareth brings a radically different
approach to peace. While we go around everywhere
looking for peace, Jesus Christ gives it away!

> *Jesus answered and said unto him...Peace
> I leave with you, my peace I give unto you:
> not as the world giveth, give I unto you. John
> 14:23, 27.*

> *Jesus answered and said...Come unto me,
> all ye that labour and are heavy laden, and I
> will give you rest. Matthew 11:25, 28.*

Well that's different! The peace that Jesus so freely gives away is one of the reasons people were—and still are—so drawn to him. Jesus *is* peace. Jesus Christ is wisdom, and peace actually comes from wisdom!

> *Christ the power of God, and the wisdom of God. 1 Corinthians 1:24.*

> *Happy is the man that findeth wisdom...all her paths are peace. Proverbs 3:13, 17.*

> *For unto us a child is born, unto us a son is given: and the government shall be upon his shoulder: and his name shall be called Wonderful, Counsellor, The mighty God, The everlasting Father, The Prince of Peace. Of the increase of his government and peace there shall be no end. Isaiah 9:6-7.*

> *For he is our peace. Ephesians 2:14.*

Wise decisions create peaceful situations. For example, you're having a really great year at your job, with excellent pay. Instead of buying new cars, new homes, new boats and taking all those vacations you always wanted to exotic places, you decide to pay off debt on old cars, your old home, credit cards, and save one fifth of your earnings, for a rainy day.

And then it happens. That rainy day comes along. Suddenly, you and your whole country are passing through a lean season. Some call it recession, others call it depression, but you are able to sleep peacefully in your own home and feed your family, because you got out of debt and saved a little money. Your wise choice during the years of plenty gave you and your family peace, during the lean years.

> *Joseph answered Pharaoh, saying, It is not in me: God shall give Pharaoh an answer of <u>peace</u>...Now therefore let Pharaoh look out a man <u>discreet and wise</u>, and set him over the land of Egypt. Let Pharaoh do this, and let him appoint officers over the land, and take up the fifth part of the land of Egypt in the seven plenteous years...And that food shall be for store to the land against the seven years of famine, which shall be in the land of Egypt; that the land perish not through the famine. Genesis 41:16, 33-34, 36.*

It is really nice to have a wise leader during your years of plenty, isn't it? Enough said.

Some of us have heard the legend of King Solomon's wisdom? Well can you guess what followed King Solomon around?

> *And the LORD gave Solomon wisdom, as he promised him: and there was <u>peace</u> between Hiram and Solomon. 1 Kings 5:12.*

> *For he had dominion over all the region*
> *on this side the river, from Tiphsah even*
> *to Azzah, over all the kings on this side the*
> *river: and he had peace on all sides round*
> *about him. 1 Kings 4:24.*

Peace is wisdom's sidekick. Since Christ is all wisdom, Jesus isn't worried that he might run out of his peace stockpile! He gives peace freely, to whoever will receive it. But here is where it gets tricky. Now that you have obtained a deposit of Jesus' peace, that profound calm and tranquility that he so effortlessly possesses, what comes next?

What are you supposed to do with it?

Chapter 12

Enjoy the peace. Then give it away.

You and I were made for this! *Give it away.* Don't get all worked up, as if you are going to run out of peace or something! Listen to Jesus' words from the gospels of Matthew and John,

> *Freely ye have received, freely give. Matthew 10:8.*

> *Peace I leave with you, my peace I give unto you: not as the world giveth, give I unto you. Let not your heart be troubled, neither let it be afraid. John 14:27.*

Your "peace" source—Jesus—has peace that never ends, so relax! Peace is like a candle that lights another candle. It neither gets extinguished, nor depleted.

The passage above talks about a peace from Jesus that is different from the peace that the world gives. What is the big difference? To see this clearly, we will look at peace, as the world gives it.

World peace comes from the outside in. Laws are made to establish a police force and special training

forces of all kinds to literally "keep the peace." Firefight-
ers heroically dash around putting out fires in the dead of
night, so that the people can sleep peacefully till morning.

But if the police, the SWAT team, the fire depart-
ment or ambulance services are disabled for as little as
twenty-four hours, "the peace" instantly goes away!
Where did all that peace go? Along with those services!
We have all witnessed chaos, violence and mass lootings
break out when riots or natural disasters occur. Remember hurricane Katrina and most recently, tropical storm
Sandy.

That same "outside in" peace is on display when
people choose what they would assume are peaceful
neighborhoods to live in, peaceful jobs to work in, or ac-
cumulate as much money as they can. Hard drugs, heavy
alcohol drinking and tobacco use buy others a brief period of peace, from tortured unrest. But that peace vanish-
es when the junkie comes down off the drugs, or the fat
bank balance dwindles. Or "That awful family!" moves
next door.

In other words, "World peace" is fickle. You search
for it, consume it and then poof! It is gone.

By contrast, *Jesus' peace is from the inside out.* You
carry his peace around with you, wherever you go. You
are a peace source, creating peaceful places! Your peace is
therefore independent of where you are. On some occasions, you will actually seek out a place of chaos, to bring
peace to it!

I cannot count the number of times someone has
walked up to me and told me how peaceful being around

me makes them feel. This is surprising a lot of times, because I am not doing anything that, at least in my mind, qualifies as holy activity. In fact, a lot of times I am doing what I consider to be the most ordinary of tasks. For example, my young sons get peace from watching me *eat*. They just stand around watching, grinning from ear to ear! Go figure.

The big difference is that "Jesus' peace" is faithful. You are a peacemaker, and your peace is with you always.

> *Blessed are the peacemakers: for they shall be called the children of God. Matthew 5:9.*

> *Jesus came and spake unto them, saying...lo, I am with you alway, even unto the end of the world. Matthew 28:18, 20.*

So you are actually a peace generator. But as God's peace instrument, how do we give his peace away? Well, there's an app for that! Jesus told us very clearly how to do this.

> *And into whatsoever house ye enter, first say, Peace be to this house. And if the son of peace be there, your peace shall rest upon it: if not, it shall turn to you again. Luke 10:5-6.*

> *And when ye come into an house, salute it. And if the house be worthy, let your peace*

> *come upon it: but if it be not worthy, let your*
> *peace return to you. Matthew 10:12-13.*

Give your peace to any house that will accept it. Jesus did not give a suggestion, he gave a direct command! Actually, it was the first thing we are instructed to do when we get there! Some will say this was only done when the disciples went out to preach the gospel. True, but you should leave your home every day with the intent of preaching the gospel to *somebody*.

> *For you, the people that you meet each day*
> *are the "house" Jesus was speaking of.*

So the Luke version sounds a little dated to you, like you are some first century guru with a long flowing white beard, or something? There are more contemporary ways of doing the same thing—Matthew gives you the latitude to change the "salute," without affecting its intent. Take a leaf from the Jamaicans. You may not be able to catch them in a foot race, but you can...

Strike a hip-looking pose with a peace hand symbol and say "Peace!" You'll probably get a laugh, maybe even start a new fashion trend, it really doesn't matter how you do it, just give the good stuff away! There is somebody out there who desperately needs it. It is as simple as that. You are doing something profound in the spiritual world with what appears to be a simple insignificant gesture.

In fact stand up right now and say "Peace!" before you get embarrassed and change your mind. You have just, in true "Word before wisdom" fashion, applied the *how* of peace making. But what exactly are you doing, other than making people feel content? What is the wisdom behind this word, and *why* is it such a big deal? This answer may surprise you.

Peace is the best way to introduce Jesus.

Chapter 13

Peace is the best way to introduce Jesus! The person who experiences it suddenly understands what the kingdom of God is like. For a moment, they actually *get* the essence of Jesus. What better time is there to introduce him?

> *Jesus answered them, Do ye now believe? These things I have spoken unto you, that <u>in me</u> ye might have <u>peace</u>. John 16:31, 33.*

> *For he is our peace. Ephesians 2:13-14.*

> *For the kingdom of God is not meat and drink; but righteousness, and peace, and joy in the Holy Ghost. Romans 14:17.*

A mind that experiences Jesus' brand of peace even for a few moments is, for those moments, a mind that can actually *listen* to you! Think about a chaotic mind, with a bunch of conflicting thoughts all jumbled up in it. How on earth is such a mind going to pay attention to anything you say?

> *A double minded man is unstable in all his ways. James 1:8.*
>
> *Some things hard to be understood, which they that are unlearned and unstable wrest, as they do also the other scriptures. 2 Peter 3:16.*

Now, watch that change, as you deposit your peace on a place. Suddenly, you get undivided attention! Cell phones get switched off, TVs turned off, and a lot of times your audience marvels, as they taste true peace for the first time. In that moment, they see a truth that cannot be denied. They are now ready to consider and *perceive* the rest of what you have to say.

This type of "peace making" was commonplace among the New Testament apostles. They gave peace away in obedience to Jesus' specific instructions on the subject. Let's catalogue the New Testament books that give away peace, while providing "God information," in what was undoubtedly a standard practice.

> Matthew 10:12-13—And when ye come into an house, salute it. And if the house be worthy, let your peace come upon it: but if it be not worthy, let your peace return to you.
>
> Mark 4:39—And he arose, and rebuked the wind, and said unto the sea, Peace, be still. And the wind ceased, and there was a great calm.

Luke 10:5—And into whatsoever house ye enter, first say, Peace be to this house.

John 14:27—Peace I leave with you, my peace I give unto you: not as the world giveth, give I unto you.

John 20:20—Jesus and stood in the midst, and saith unto them, Peace be unto you.

Romans 1:7—Grace to you and peace from God our Father, and the Lord Jesus Christ.

1 Corinthians 1:3—Grace *be* unto you, and peace, from God our Father, and *from* the Lord Jesus Christ.

2 Corinthians 1:2—Grace *be* to you and peace from God our Father, and *from* the Lord Jesus Christ.

Galatians 1:3—Grace *be* to you and peace from God the Father, and *from* our Lord Jesus Christ,

Ephesians 1:2—Grace *be* to you, and peace, from God our Father, and *from* the Lord Jesus Christ.

Philippians 1:2—Grace *be* unto you, and

peace, from God our Father, and *from* the Lord Jesus Christ.

Colossians 1:2—To the saints and faithful brethren in Christ which are at Colosse: Grace *be* unto you, and peace, from God our Father and the Lord Jesus Christ.

1 Thessalonians 1:1—Grace *be* unto you, and peace, from God our Father, and the Lord Jesus Christ.

2 Thessalonians 1:2—Grace unto you, and peace, from God our Father and the Lord Jesus Christ.

1 Timothy 1:2—Unto Timothy, *my* own son in the faith: Grace, mercy, *and* peace, from God our Father and Jesus Christ our Lord.

2 Timothy 1:2—To Timothy, *my* dearly beloved son: Grace, mercy, *and* peace, from God the Father and Christ Jesus our Lord.

Philemon 1:3—Grace to you, and peace, from God our Father and the Lord Jesus Christ.

James 3:18—And the fruit of righteousness is sown in peace of them that make peace.

1 Peter 1:2—Grace unto you, and peace, be multiplied.

2 Peter 1:2—Grace and peace be multiplied unto you through the knowledge of God, and of Jesus our Lord,

2 John 1:3—Grace be with you, mercy, *and* peace, from God the Father, and from the Lord Jesus Christ, the Son of the Father, in truth and love.

3 John 1:14—Peace *be* to thee.

Jude 1:2—Mercy unto you, and peace, and love, be multiplied.

Revelation 1:4-5—Grace *be* unto you, and peace, from him which is, and which was, and which is to come; and from the seven Spirits which are before his throne; And from Jesus Christ.

Wow! Now that is quite an impressive list, if I may say so myself! How could we have missed this obviously important instruction? The answer is really quite simple. We have not read the Bible like an instruction manual. Instead, we have opted to read the Bible like a history book. This makes us see and yet not perceive the relevance of what we see, hear and yet not understand its instructions, as useful life tools from within its pages pass us by.

Did you think "Peace be unto you!" was simply the secular greeting style in Jesus' day? Not so, my friend. They were carrying out specific instructions from Jesus Christ himself! As we saw in the passages above, peace was used for the benefit of both Christians and non-Christians alike.

This peace instruction was so effective at growing the Christian church that Moslems, members of a religion which started after Christianity, saw its effect, adopted it as their doctrine, and have continued to use it to this very day! "*As Salaam Alaikum*" means "Peace be upon you." Piggybacking off the peace blessing, this religion also started to spread, like wildfire.

So, *everyone* is supposed to soak up peace, in that instant experiencing what God has already decreed is "the real normal." Primed after this reality check, it is time to listen to what God has to say. So, you have now successfully primed your prospective audience to lend you their ears.

What story are you going tell them?

Chapter 14

Tell them the story of how you got your peace. The story of your peace is the *gospel*. There is no more powerful way to win people for Jesus Christ than your personal testimony.

> *And I heard a loud voice saying in heaven, Now is come salvation, and strength, and the kingdom of our God, and the power of his Christ: for the accuser of our brethren is cast down, which accused them before our God day and night. And they overcame him by the blood of the Lamb, and by the word of their testimony. Revelation 12:10-11.*

The truth of a personal testimony cannot be contested as a theory. It speaks for itself. This is what makes it so powerful and why Satan hates it so much. Your God story is an *experience*, not a teaching. And the best part of your story is that it can never be taken away from you. It is your story after all.

But it is your responsibility to have a peace story to tell! Whatever specifics your God story contains, it will have three components arranged in sequence, as there is no other way to obtain real peace.

First, there will be God's Word that you obeyed. Next up is the wisdom that came to you after your obedience. Lastly, with wisdom comes peace. Never forget that sequence; word, wisdom, peace. The last two are the very tasty fruits of obedience to the first.

> *The wisdom that is from above is first pure, then peaceable, gentle, and easy to be intreated, full of mercy and good fruits, without partiality, and without hypocrisy. James 3:17.*

> *O taste and see that the LORD is good. Psalm 34:8.*

As I stated earlier, your peace story is the gospel. That probably sounds a little odd to you, so we'll go directly to the source and do some fact checking. What exactly does the Bible say is the gospel?

> *<u>The word of the Lord endureth for ever.</u> And this is the word which by the gospel is preached unto you. 1 Peter 1:25.*

> *And I saw another angel fly in the midst of heaven, having the everlasting gospel to preach unto them that dwell on the earth, and to every nation, and kindred, and*

tongue, and people, Saying with a loud voice,
<u>Fear God, and give glory to him</u>; for the hour
of his judgment is come. Revelation 14:6-7.

And Jesus went about all the cities and
villages, teaching in their synagogues, and
preaching the <u>gospel of the kingdom</u>, and
healing every sickness and every disease
among the people. Matthew 9:35.

Gospel means "good news." The gospel is the unchanged word of God, or God's instructions, which in turn is the same thing as the spirit of Jesus Christ. Obeying those instructions gets you the kingdom of God, with its contained wisdom, peace and rest. This has always been and will always be the gospel.

The gospel is not our belief in Jesus' death and resurrection only—that is *part* of the gospel. As seen in the scripture above, Jesus himself preached the gospel while he was still alive on earth and had not yet told the general public that he would die for the remission of all sins, and the salvation of mankind. So what "gospel of the kingdom" was he preaching?

He was preaching the same gospel that Moses got from Mount Sinai, summarized in the very first commandment—you shall have no other gods before me. It was the same gospel that as an old man, King Solomon summarized in the last chapter of Ecclesiastes—Fear God, and keep his commandments. It was the same "everlasting gospel" that the angel in the passage above declared—Fear God, obey him and inherit his kingdom, along with its contained wisdom and peace.

> *And God spake all these words, saying, I am the LORD thy God, which have brought thee out of the land of Egypt, out of the house of bondage. Thou shalt have no other gods before me. Exodus 20:1-3.*

> *Let us hear the conclusion of the whole matter: Fear God, and keep his commandments: for this is the whole duty of man. For God shall bring every work into judgment, with every secret thing, whether it be good, or whether it be evil. Ecclesiastes 12:13-14.*

Fear God and obey his instructions. Then God, as your father, and his kingdom with all its contained wisdom and peace becomes yours. Is that not how you got your peace? Again note the sequence; the word first, then wisdom and peace. Therefore, this is the very same gospel you preach by telling your peace story. But those who do not obey God's words do not have a peace story to tell. They also have a very different father.

> *Jesus said unto them…Why do ye not understand my speech? even because ye cannot hear my word. Ye are of your father the devil, and the lusts of your father ye will do. John 8:42-44.*

But with whom was he grieved forty years? was it not with them that had sinned, whose carcases fell in the wilderness? And to whom sware he that they should not enter into his rest, but to them that believed not?...

...Let us therefore fear, lest, a promise being left us of entering into his rest, any of you should seem to come short of it. For unto us was the gospel preached, <u>as well as unto them</u>: but the word preached did not profit them, not being mixed with faith in them that heard it. For we which have believed do enter into rest. Hebrews 3:17-18; 4:1-3.

Therefore to him that knoweth to do good, and doeth it not, to him it is sin. James 4:17.

As you can see from the Hebrews passage above, the gospel was preached to the Israelites in the wilderness! But they did not obtain peace, because they chose to not obey the instructions of God. Like them, we also get outcomes based on our choices. I don't know about you, but I believe in a certain credo when it comes to God's prophecies. Never get caught on the wrong end of a prophecy!

So now we understand that the gospel is actually the story of how you got peace to live within you. And there is a unique advantage to carrying your peace around with you. Like a well-packed suitcase, you can travel around with it. This makes you a peace maker wherever you go. God really likes that!

> *It is written, How beautiful are the feet of them that preach the gospel of peace, and bring glad tidings of good things! Romans 10:15.*

> *Stand therefore, having your loins girt about with truth...and your feet shod with the preparation of the gospel of peace. Ephesians 6:14, 15.*

So to recap, what have we learned in this "peace" section? To summarize, in two or three paragraphs:

Your obedience to God's word is rewarded with wisdom. With wisdom comes perfect peace. Peace is a light that attracts the attention of others. Give morsels of peace away—it is *fish bait*. If your peace is accepted, it becomes a ministry tool—you've hooked your fish!

If your peace is rejected, it returns to you. The fish didn't take the bait, but don't worry about it. Go someplace else and throw out your bait—further upstream, a fish will bite. If your peace is desired and sought by your audience, tell your "peace" story. Yours is a story of obedience to God, and its reward. *That is the gospel.*

Offer the same pathway to your attentive audience. Nine times out of ten they will take it! After a taste of true peace, who wouldn't? It's hard to go back to life in a chaos bowl and call that "normal." Congratulations, preacher! You've just won your first Christian convert. Have you any idea what you've just become?

You are now God's instrument. You have just become a fisher of men.

> *Jesus, walking by the sea of Galilee, saw two brethren, Simon called Peter, and Andrew his brother, casting a net into the sea: for they were fishers. And he saith unto them, Follow me, and I will make you fishers of men. Matthew 4:18-19.*

THE GRACE OF GOD

My grace is sufficient for thee.
2 Corinthians 12:9.

Chapter 15

Did you notice that in most of the passages where peace is mentioned, the word "grace" is close by? In this section, we will explore in detail the concept of God's grace.

> Grace: Unmerited divine assistance given humans for their regeneration or sanctification—Merriam-Webster dictionary.

In its simplest definition, grace is unmerited favor, or privilege. I think the key word here is unmerited. Grace is never earned; therefore it is not a reward, neither is it a wage. Grace is an unearned *gift*. Fun! And God gives away lots of it.

> *For all things are for your sakes, that the <u>abundant grace</u> might through the thanksgiving of many redound to the glory of God. 2 Corinthians 4:15.*

> *That in the ages to come he might shew the exceeding riches of his grace in his kindness toward us through Christ Jesus. For by grace*

are ye saved through faith; and that <u>not of</u>
<u>yourselves</u>: it is the gift of God. Ephesians 2:7-8.

Everyone receives grace from God. You did not earn the right to wake up this morning; that privilege was given to you. You did not earn the right to be born, nor did you earn the right to interact with the world in a thousand wonderful ways—to see a butterfly, watch a beautiful sunset, feel a cool breeze, walk, talk, eat, smile—you name it. Grace is how you are alive, reading this page today.

But unto <u>every one of us</u> is given grace
according to the measure of the gift of Christ.
Wherefore he saith, When he ascended up on
high, he led captivity captive, and gave gifts
unto men. Ephesians 4:7-8.

And of his fulness <u>have all we received</u>, and
grace for grace. For the law was given by Moses,
but grace and truth came by Jesus Christ. John
1:16-17.

One striking example of God's amazing grace toward us is *time*. We are given time to correct mistakes, and get better. This grace is so universal, so profound and yet so often ignored by most people, that I feel compelled to discuss it in more detail.

Time is best described as a countdown to the kingdom of God. The steady progression of time is measured by the passage of *years*. Therefore a year once passed never comes round again. The year 1999 is never coming back; it is one and done. But what about the other measures of time? What do seconds, minutes, hours, days, weeks and months all have in common, which differentiates them from the year?

They are all cyclical.

Unlike years, all other measures of time come around again and again. 5 o'clock on Friday evening officially starts the weekend for most people, and the popular acronym of the day is T.G.I.F.—Thank God it's Friday! Then several activities later, it's Sunday night, and Monday morning is the most dreaded morning ever! Slog your way through the week and suddenly, it is 5 o'clock on Friday again! And the beat goes on.

Why does Monday keep coming back, over and over again? Why does a broken watch tell the right time, twice a day? Why do we keep having New Year's Day and a whole new set of resolutions in January, most of which we break by February?

Because each repeated measure of time demonstrates the wonderful gift of God's grace.

Chapter 16

Earlier on, we said that time counts down to God's kingdom. Let's examine the count down, with an emphasis on the passage of years.

Years steadily march forward, until the kingdom of God comes, with Jesus Christ returning as the supreme king of heaven and earth. Later on, time is done, and eternity begins. Therefore, saying "the year 2012" is the same thing as saying "2012 years closer to the return of Jesus Christ as king, in the kingdom of God."

The whole time business is really a Jesus Christ countdown. And just so that there's no mistake about who really gives "time" meaning, Jesus Christ is the same yardstick by which the passage of years is measured!

B.C. means Before Christ. A.D. is Anno Domini, Latin for "In the year of our Lord." C.E. stands for The Common Era and B.C.E. for Before the Common Era. C.E. and B.C.E. represent a political name change, to appease people who disagree with the idea of Jesus Christ as Lord. But what or more correctly who symbolizes the start of the Common Era? *Jesus Christ,* same as in the older, more widely known B.C. and A.D. system.

So, God the Father firmly ties his son Jesus to the whole spectrum of time. The Father also makes sure that Jesus Christ is glorified as Lord, whether people like it, understand it or not. We acknowledge Jesus Christ's lordship every time we say what year it is! But why is the Father so insistent on tying Jesus to time?

Because time is a measure of God's grace.
And all grace comes through Jesus Christ.

Do you remember that forest fire story, from a few chapters ago? Let me recap it for you...

Think of you being in a large forest fire...Suddenly somebody comes running up to you with a precise map of the only pathway out of that forest. He tells you to follow him and do exactly what he says and does if you want to live...

That is the story of your life, so far. Because though you may not know it, you're in a forest fire, and you've been in it since the day you were conceived. You and I were born into it, and the day we leave this fiery forest is the day we die. You can choose to leave the forest alive, or charred and very dead. Either way, we are currently going through hell on earth, and Jesus is our only hope of getting out of here alive.

The sorrows of death compassed me, and the
pains of hell gat hold upon me: I found trouble
and sorrow. Then called I upon the name of
the LORD; O LORD, I beseech thee, deliver
my soul. Gracious is the LORD, and righteous;
yea, our God is merciful. Psalm 116:3-5.

I foresaw the Lord always before my face, for he is on my right hand, that I should not be moved: Therefore did my heart rejoice, and my tongue was glad; moreover also my flesh shall rest in hope: Because thou wilt not leave my soul in hell, neither wilt thou suffer thine Holy One to see corruption. Thou hast made known to me the ways of life. Acts2:25-28.

I cried by reason of mine affliction unto the LORD, and he heard me; out of the belly of hell cried I, and thou heardest my voice. Jonah 2:2.

Jesus Christ is the person who came running up to you and asked you to follow him. He came through that fire for you! By grace he chose to save you, at great personal sacrifice and pain. *You did not earn the right to be saved.* Do you see the magnitude of God's grace? Without Jesus, you and I are toast! Do you now see why God the Father insists his son's amazing grace and sacrifice is given the place of honor it deserves?

Let this mind be in you, which was also in Christ Jesus: Who, being in the form of God, thought it not robbery to be equal with God: But made himself of no reputation, and took upon him the form of a servant, and was made in the likeness of men: And being found in fashion as a man, he humbled himself, and *became obedient unto death, even the death of the cross. Wherefore God also hath highly exalted him, and given him a name which is above every name: That at the name of Jesus every knee should bow, of things in heaven, and things in earth, and things under the earth; And <u>that every tongue</u> should confess that Jesus Christ is Lord, to the glory of God the Father. Philippians 2:5-11.*

God the Father takes it very personally when his son's grace-filled sacrifice is not given its rightful place of honor, and yet…

God *still* gives us another day, despite the terrible things some people say about Jesus! One more chance at a new beginning, we are offered a fresh start, a do over, a second opportunity to make a first impression. One more shot at choosing to do God's Word, with every repeated moment. One more gift of time, to grab a hold of salvation and live.

But most of us are not even aware that currently, we exist under grace.

Chapter 17

So, most of us squander the grace we have been given. But how could we knowingly do such a thing? Ironically, it is because of the truth we have been taught about grace.

We have been coached thoroughly on the fact that grace's gifts are not earned, so we can't boast we earned them. We have understood the gift of grace is to be consumed—it's a free gift after all; accept it, and enjoy it. But is that really all there is to it? Does grace serve any purpose other than to make me happy? Let's walk through an example and see if this is indeed the case.

A young orphan walks the streets with no food to eat. Let's call him "Christian." You have compassion on the young boy, and bring him into your home as your own child. Obviously, your dream is for him to grow up responsibly and learn to be a man in a home filled with love, rather than the bitter world of fighting, of scavenging for rotting scraps of food in the trash, and, most likely, a premature violent death.

So, Christian is given warm meals lovingly cooked by "Mom," a cozy bed to sleep in, and a loving family. But strangely enough, he never clears away his plates, never helps wash or dry the dishes and in fact never cleans or tidies up after himself. All your other children routinely do these necessary household chores.

When asked why, the little fellow replies "I live here by grace. Didn't you tell me to enjoy grace? I don't enjoy cleaning my room, washing the dishes, or brushing my teeth. Yuck! But I *really* like to eat, play and sleep! So that's what I do. I eat, I play and I sleep!"

Now, what do you say to a response like that?

> *You tell young Christian why you gave him grace.*

You explain grace, from your perspective. That grace does not exempt him from household responsibilities, but actually creates a safe haven for him to learn those responsibilities. That grace is a prelude to a dream, a dream of him, and who he could become.

> *God is able to make all grace abound toward you; that ye, always having <u>all</u> sufficiency in <u>all</u> things, may abound to <u>every</u> good work. 2 Corinthians 9:8.*

> *Eye hath not seen, nor ear heard, neither have entered into the heart of man, the things which God hath prepared for them that love him. 1 Corinthians 2:9.*

You tell him that the same grace he currently enjoys is big enough to cover the mistakes he will make, as he learns different household chores and takes on his mantle of responsibility.

> *My grace is sufficient for thee. 2 Corinthians 12:9.*

You show him that these chores are as much part of this home as the love, laughter, food and rest that he currently enjoys here. Those instructions are what will make him grow up to be just like you and, with your other children, inherit your household.

> *I commend you to God, and to the word of his grace, which is able to <u>build you up</u>, and to give you an <u>inheritance</u> among all them which are sanctified. Acts 20:32.*

Now, it's up to young Christian. What kind of man will he grow up to be?

That depends on him. Grace comes with responsibility and still requires committed action on Christian's part. Grace is defined as divine unmerited *assistance* for sanctification, remember? Grace will give him an environment to thrive in and grow, but grace alone will not make him a man. That part he has to choose for himself.

> *What will he decide?*

Chapter 18

So, everybody on the planet has received grace from God, but this does not make grace an aimless whim. If looked at closely, grace is a tangible demonstration of God's faith in you, and the greatness you can achieve if you choose!

> The <u>grace of our Lord</u> was exceeding abundant <u>with faith</u> and love which is in Christ Jesus. This is a faithful saying, and worthy of all acceptation. 1 Timothy 1:14-15.
>
> Peace be to the brethren, and love <u>with faith, from God the Father</u> and the Lord Jesus Christ. Ephesians 6:23.

God has faith in—*me*? I don't know about you, but that blows me away! With all my inconsistencies, incredibly, God's answer to that question is a resounding yes! It is the reason he gave us such amazing grace in the first place. But what *will* we choose, and what happens to grace then?

If I choose to learn under his grace, God's grace stays with me for ever. If I, as a "young Christian," decide to follow the rules of God's household, God's grace helps me grow into a Godly man. This is the day I spiritually turn eighteen, get proudly introduced to everyone as co-owner of God's house, and partner with God in maintaining his wonderful household. This is what it means to reign with him.

> *Blessed and holy is he that hath part in the first resurrection: on such the second death hath no power, but they shall be priests of God and of Christ, and shall reign with him a thousand years. Revelation 20:6.*

All those years under grace have paid off—my training has made me useful! But everything I have become has been through the help of grace. Grace defines who I am, and is seen in everything I will become. In other words, God's grace has become a permanent part of my story and never leaves me.

If I choose not to learn under his grace, God's grace has an expiration date. That is the day I "tap out," or run out of time. It also is the day I turn eighteen. Suddenly, adult life starts, real life demands are made and I cannot meet those demands, because I never learned how. What is to become of me? Once again, let's walk through an example, the real life story of a young king.

The year is 1936 and the country of Great Britain is in turmoil. The newly crowned King Edward VIII is considering the unthinkable. Young King Edward is determined to marry an American divorcee, a certain Mrs. Wallis Simpson.

Part of the job of being the British king was being the head of the Anglican Church. The Bible states that marrying a divorcee is adultery. How could the head of the church do such a thing? This caused such concern that the British Prime Minister, Stanley Baldwin tried to talk him out of it. Sir Winston Churchill tried to talk him out of it. But their pleas were to no avail. King Edward's mind was made up.

The country watched in dismay. Here was a British king, bent on doing something that a British king could not do! Based on his choice, there was really only one course of action left open to King Edward. To give up his crown, and be king no more.

So, the king gave up his kingdom and married Mrs. Simpson. All his childhood training on how to take on the responsibility of being his country's king ended up being for nothing. But that waste had everything to do with Edward's attitude and choices. There had been early warning signs that Edward would be a problem child for his kingdom.

King Edward had done several other things that were outside of his job description. He threw wild extravagant parties and destroyed a lot of the old precious trees that had been part of the British landscape for centuries. Regarding Edward, it is said that Edward's own Assistant Private Secretary, Alan Lascelles, had told the British Prime Minister as early as 1927: "I can't help thinking that the best thing that could happen to him, and to the country, would be for him to break his neck."

What do you think will happen to you when you turn eighteen in God's kingdom, with different ideas of how his kingdom should be run?

> *Ye are the salt of the earth: but if the salt have lost his savour, wherewith shall it be salted? it is thenceforth good for nothing, but to be cast out, and to be trodden under foot of men. Matthew 5:13.*

> *If a man abide not in me, he is cast forth as a branch, and is withered; and men gather them, and cast them into the fire, and they are burned. John 15:6.*

Jesus Christ's words not mine—don't shoot the messenger! The bottom line is if you have squandered the grace you were given, you lose your amazing gift, and grace goes away! For God's purposes, you have made yourself absolutely useless. What a waste!

Let's take a last scenario. What if I choose to do all God asks me to do except for just one habit close to my heart that I choose not to give up? For the sake of this example, let's use stealing. For some strange reason, I have chosen to see stealing as an art form— pick-pocketing, shoplifting, credit card identity theft etc. God has repeatedly insisted I stop this habit, but I refuse to do so. After all, it's the *only* bad thing I do.

As an adult, how long will it be before I steal from the wrong person and meet my end, rotting away inside the four walls of a jail cell or six feet under the ground? Most of you reading are thinking "Well, that doesn't apply to me. I don't steal! I'm a *good* person!" Are you sure about that?

> *Will a man rob God? Yet ye have robbed me. But ye say, Wherein have we robbed thee? In tithes and offerings. Ye are cursed with a curse: for ye have robbed me, even this whole nation. Malachi 3:8-9.*

Things are not always as they seem. When was the last time you paid your tithes? But putting robbery aside for a minute and looking at the big picture, what keeps you out of heaven—the size of your sin, or your resistance to changing it?

> *And a certain ruler asked him, saying, Good Master, what shall I do to inherit eternal life? And Jesus said unto him, Why callest thou me good? none is good, save one, that is, God. Thou knowest the commandments, Do not commit adultery, Do not kill, Do not steal, Do not bear false witness, Honour thy father and thy mother. And he said, All these have I kept from my youth up. Now when Jesus heard these things, he said unto him, Yet lackest thou <u>one thing</u>: sell all that thou*

> *hast, and distribute unto the poor, and thou*
> *shalt have treasure in heaven: and come,*
> *follow me. And when he heard this, he was*
> *very sorrowful: for he was very rich. And*
> *when Jesus saw that he was very sorrowful,*
> *he said, How hardly shall they that have*
> *riches enter into the kingdom of God! Luke*
> *18:18-24.*

The man in this story had done everything that we today call decent—he had obeyed the rules and made a fortune through honest hard work. Sounds like the American dream to me! But Jesus asked this man to give away his hard-earned money to poor people that didn't earn it! What?? Forgive me, I almost hesitate to say it in front of my Republican friends, but doesn't Jesus sound suspiciously like a democrat socialist?

Do you even agree that this man choosing not to give away all his hard-earned money to the poor is a sin at all? But that decision was going to cost him the kingdom of God. The man's sadness as he walked away indicated that he knew it would too, but *he just couldn't let go of that one thing!* His deliberate choice to disobey was all that mattered.

One persistently chosen area of disobedience in a sea of good behavior still ends in the same result as if you were not under grace at all. The rich man's story is told in three of the four Gospels, so it must be extremely important. But if later on that rich man changed his mind, God's grace would be sufficient for him to make heaven. As we have learned all section long, time is grace.

However a "coming of age" day is coming. So, when is your coming of age day, the special day you turn eighteen that I've been repeatedly talking about?

The day you turn eighteen is the day that you die.

Chapter 19

Well! Grace has turned out to be quite the topic, hasn't it? To me, grace is like Pandora's Box; the deeper I delve, the more new things I pull out of it! Here's a brief recap of the things we have learned about grace thus far:

Grace is the unearned gift that assists, but does not do all the work for you.

God gives us grace in the belief that we will use it to become better—making grace God's statement of faith in us.

Since we need time to improve, *time itself is grace.* Improve over time and keep the grace gift; misuse time, and grace is taken from you.

There is no other way given to obtain any grace, but by Jesus Christ, the Son of God. There is no other way to *keep* grace, but by accepting Jesus Christ, the Word and wisdom of God, as Lord.

Good! Now to wrap things up, let us discuss how we recognize grace in people, and how we put all the grace theory we have learned into practice, in today's world.

There are actually two ways to recognize a grace-filled person. The first is by observing the effects of grace on that individual person. Grace shows up in a person as their glory. We will talk about glory in more detail in the next section.

The second way to recognize a gracious person is by their grace towards other people. We should be able to recognize these "grace symptoms" in a person, when we see them:

> *A person full of grace routinely gives people gifts they did not earn.* This type of gift is not a payment, neither is it a reward for good behavior.

> *The grace gift given usually helps the recipient learn something new that makes them better.* This means it is not a "one and done gift" such as food, or a "repeat use, basic necessity gift" like a shirt.

> *A person of grace is patient with people.* Patience should never be mistaken for tolerance of bad behavior.

> *What then? shall we sin, because we are not*

under the law, but under grace? God forbid.
Romans 6:15.

The gracious person waits because he or she has faith in you, believing you will change for the better, if given time and help.

If gracious people get their wish, they make people better. If a grace-filled person gets his or her wish, the people around them change for the better and ultimately become gracious too.

If gracious people do not get their wish, they are removed from the recipient of their grace. If grace is ignored and consumed in vain, one of two things will ultimately happen. Either the fruitless receiver of grace leaves the circle of influence of the gracious person, or the person of grace leaves to a new location.

So, if a gracious man has his way in me, he makes me gracious as well. This means people will see grace in me, as they recognize my grace symptoms:

I will routinely give people gifts they did not earn.

My gifts will help people learn something good and new.

I will be patient with people. This will be with grace, not tolerance.

If my grace is not in vain, it gets multiplied, showing up in other people.

If my grace is ineffective, I will be removed from fruitless recipients of my grace.

This is the grace of God and how it looks in you and I. God's holiness cannot be compromised, but grace creates a buffer zone for us, giving us time and help to become holy with God. I love the way I heard it put by a good friend of mine. In true NFL football speak, she said: "grace runs interference between us and God." Jesus Christ is our buffer zone, our grace. Do not let his grace be in vain.

We then, as workers together with him, beseech you also that ye receive not the grace of God in vain... 2 Corinthians 6:1.

...For the law was given by Moses, but grace and truth came by Jesus Christ. John 1:17.

This ends the grace section. Next up—the glory of God.

THE GLORY OF GOD

Fear God, and give glory to him.
Revelation 14:7.

Chapter 20

Glory is interesting.

Almost everybody enjoys glory when they see it, but a lot of people are not willing to go through what it takes to get it.

> *A woman when she is in travail hath sorrow, because her hour is come: but as soon as she is delivered of the child, she remembereth no more the anguish, for joy that a man is born into the world. John 16:21.*

It's like the relationship between pregnancy and a newborn baby. People love the baby, but most don't enjoy the pregnancy. And *nobody* enjoys the childbirth. Hate the process, love the result.

So what is glory, exactly?

> Glory: Great honor, praise, or distinction accorded by common consent; renown—The American Heritage Dictionary of the English Language.

Glory is any good thing that attracts and pleases a crowd.

Glory is a good thing so remarkable that it makes you instantly want to tell somebody else about it. The news spreads, creates new admirers, and the glory grows. Therefore with glory, the more people come and admire the good happening, the more the glory.

Glory can have many very different presentations. Miracles are a glory to those who perform them. The bravery of firemen, feats of great strength, outstanding sporting or academic achievement, an inspiring speech, even remarkable musical ability are all examples of glory. A new-born baby is glorious, and gives glory to the proud parents.

Given this understanding, we have all witnessed glory, in one form or another, because we have all seen a good, noteworthy event or person, at least once. Glory could be Michael Jordan, timelessly airborne in a basketball dunk, or your grandmother and her great cooking...yum! Glory could be an inspiring President John F. Kennedy speech, or your baby brother! As long as it is good and creates an excited buzz among people, it is glory.

So, what do we now know about glory?

We've learned that glory is an attention grabber and a crowd-pleaser. It usually refers to a single good event or activity, which can present in any number of ways. Glory increases as the crowd of admirers increases—a Michael Jordan dunk has very little glory, if he is the only one that sees it! Glory is fun, but the process to glory usually is not. And with glory as we know it so far, our audience is of people, on planet Earth. Put another way,

> *Earthly glory is admired by an earthly audience.*

Chapter 21

What is God's perspective on glory?

As definitions go, glory is essentially the same in the Bible as in our secular world. The differences are found in *what* things are regarded as glorious, and *which* crowd does the admiring. Here are some biblical examples of glory:

> And thou shalt make <u>holy garments</u> for Aaron thy brother for glory and for beauty. *Exodus 28:2.*

> The sight of the glory of the LORD was like <u>devouring fire</u> on the top of the mount in the eyes of the children of Israel. *Exodus 24:17.*

> The glory of young men is <u>their strength</u>: and the beauty of old men is the gray head. *Proverbs 20:29.*

> The <u>hoary head</u> is a crown of glory, if it be found in the way of righteousness. *Proverbs 16:31.*

Quite a diverse group isn't it? A hoary head is an old head full of grey hair. Glory is an upright senior citizen! That brings some welcome perspective to the aging process, doesn't it? But there are some biblical images of glory that are not what one would expect.

> *But if a woman have long hair, it is a glory to her: for her hair is given her for a covering. 1 Corinthians 11:15.*

> *But we glory in tribulations also. Romans 5:3.*

> *If ye be reproached for the name of Christ, happy are ye; for the spirit of glory and of God resteth upon you. 1 Peter 4:14.*

I'll be honest; I don't know what the Bible means by "long hair" glory. Why not neat, rather than long? And then, there is the glory of tribulation. Most people I know don't view tribulation as a good thing, to be spread joyfully to an applauding audience!

So, it would appear that there is another audience that assesses glory, an audience that sometimes uses different glory yardsticks than the ones we are familiar with. Who is this audience of Godly glory and where do they reside?

> *Godly glory is admired by a heavenly audience.*

This audience is of the inhabitants of heaven. This heavenly audience consists of:

1. God,
2. All heaven's angels and
3. All the holy people who have died since the beginning of the world.

Folks, that's God and lots of folks! Can you imagine such a staggering number of witnesses? Imagine that audience size, excitedly watching every single glorious event on earth! Remember, the greater the number of witnesses, the bigger the glory.

> *Wherefore seeing we also are compassed about with so great a cloud of witnesses, let us lay aside every weight. Hebrews 12:1.*

> *Ye are come unto mount Sion, and unto the city of the living God, the heavenly Jerusalem, and to an innumerable company of angels, To the general assembly and church of the firstborn, which are written in heaven, and to God the Judge of all, and to the spirits of just men made perfect, And to Jesus. Hebrews 12:22-24.*

So to recap, God's glory is also an attention grabber and a crowd-pleaser. Like earthly glory, God's glory can present in any number of ways. Unlike earthly glory,

God's glory is *always* witnessed by a huge audience; therefore the magnitude of glory is huge. And lastly, with God's glory, the primary audience is not on earth, but in heaven. This audience operates by a different set of glory rules.

We may want to familiarize ourselves with how this heavenly audience measures glory. Might as well get a jumpstart on the program, given we'll be facing all of them, after we die. To help us understand heaven's perspective, in the next two chapters we will be looking at one of the most unusual and yet, memorable biblical depictions of glory:

The glory of Jesus Christ's birth.

Chapter 22

Now the birth of Jesus Christ was on this wise… I love the Old English way Matthew starts that story. It has such a "Once upon a time" feel to it. But the particulars of this story are not your typical fairytale.

Luke starts the story with a census, and a long (at least eighty-mile) trek from Nazareth to Bethlehem, by a Jewish couple expecting a child. But when they get to their destination, their problems only get worse. The pregnant woman goes into labor.

> *And it came to pass in those days, that there went out a decree from Caesar Augustus, that all the world should be taxed…*
>
> *And Joseph also went up from Galilee, out of the city of Nazareth, into Judaea, unto the city of David, which is called Bethlehem; (because he was of the house and lineage of David:) To be taxed with Mary his espoused wife, being great with child. And so it was, that, while they were there, the days were accomplished that she should be delivered. Luke 2:1, 4-7.*

Now, I am a married man and have children of my own. I can assure you, there is nothing cute about going into labor in a strange town!

Every parent knows how much planning goes into having everything in place for childbirth. We select everything ahead of time—the right hospital, the right doctors, even the right circle of friends to run home, for any hastily forgotten items we may need. Not so, for this couple.

To make matters worse, they made this long trek at the worst possible time for them, to be *taxed*. Imagine yourself today, walking at least eighty miles from your home with your nine-month pregnant wife, to pay extra taxes, money sorely needed for your very first child's arrival into the world! Why would God allow his Son to be born under such circumstances? It happened for one simple reason:

Grace must precede glory.

Cesar Augustus' census and tax took out the human control factor. Now, only an act of God's grace could ensure a smooth labor and delivery of a healthy baby. All the expectant couple's preconceived plans were instantly thrown out the window. A young and frightened Mary must have been thinking:

Only God's grace can save me now.

So, under these circumstances, the child is born.

But, as if there was not enough of a challenge for the couple already, their worst nightmare was realized. There was not going to be a private room available for this childbirth. Mary was going to have to give birth to her firstborn son, in a stranger's barn.

And she brought forth her firstborn son, and wrapped him in swaddling clothes, and laid him in a manger; because there was no room for them in the inn. Luke 2:7.

I don't know if you caught the language used by Luke, but it cuts me to the quick. *She* wrapped him in swaddling clothes. Joseph most likely looked on helplessly. Being a carpenter in first century Galilee could not have prepared him for the process of childbirth. Like most first-time fathers I know, he was probably just standing there, terrified.

There was no one there to help them.

No Mummy to cry out to, no auntie to grab a hold of during the painful birth pangs, no cousin, no close friend, no experienced midwife to take control of the situation. Mary and Joseph were alone. So a young virgin went through labor for the first time, birthed her son, cut his umbilical cord and delivered her own afterbirth, all by herself. What training did she have, being barely more than a child herself?

> *Behold, thy cousin Elisabeth, she hath also conceived a son in her old age: and this is the <u>sixth month</u> with her, who was called barren. ...And Mary arose in those days, and went into the hill country with haste, into a city of Juda; And entered into the house of Zacharias, and saluted Elisabeth...And Mary abode with her about <u>three months</u>, and returned to her own house. Luke 1:36, 39-40, 56.*

The narrative above starts with what the angel Gabriel told Mary at Jesus conception. The rest of the passage fills in the clues of her story. Obviously, Mary watched her Cousin Elizabeth give birth to John the Baptist, Jesus Christ's cousin. That was her short, one-time training session...

> *Okay, listen up kid. You've got one shot to get this, and then it's your turn. Pay close attention! There's no do-over here. Pay attention!!*

So our Lord Jesus is wrapped up and the lost couple looked around for where to put the child. There was nowhere but the dirty eating box of the cattle and sheep in the barn. And that's where they put him.

So there you have it. We have finally caught up with...*<u>and laid him in a manger.</u>* The baby Jesus Christ was put in a manger, by his exhausted young mother, because she could find nowhere else in that stranger's barn to put him.

And this was glory?

Chapter 23

Yes. This was glory.

God's version of this same story starts quite a bit earlier. You see, in the very beginning of time, God created the universe, and everything in it.

God has a builder. This builder built the whole thing we call the universe, using God's instructions exactly as they were given; therefore he knows where everything is located, and how everything in the universe works. His name is the Holy Ghost, the Spirit of truth, or the Spirit of God.

> *In the beginning God created the heaven and the earth...And the Spirit of God moved upon the face of the waters. Genesis 1:1-2.*

> *Howbeit when he, the Spirit of truth, is come, he will guide you into all truth: for he shall not speak of himself; but whatsoever he shall hear, that shall he speak: and he will shew you things to come. John 16:13.*

> *The Holy Ghost, whom the Father will send*

in my name, he shall teach you all things.
John 14:26.

God's first instruction was "Let there be light." This was light, in every possible sense of the word. At least seven times brighter than the sun, this light also is a complete and clear understanding of how everything works, as happens in an "I have seen the light!" moment. God's builder set up the light immediately.

And God said, Let there be light: and there was light. Genesis 1:3.

The light of the sun shall be sevenfold, as the light of seven days, in the day that the LORD bindeth up the breach of his people. Isaiah 30:26.

Now, before the light came, there was a meaningless mush that existed, that had neither order nor identity. This mush is called Darkness. God separated the light from this crazy mush. He called the light "Day" to represent how things are when we see and understand clearly, and called the darkness "Night," which represents how things are when, blind in the dark mush, we cannot see and have no understanding of anything at all.

The earth was without form, and void; and darkness was upon the face of the deep... God divided the light from the darkness. And

God called the light Day, and the darkness he
called Night. Genesis 1:2, 4-5.

As a true symbol that both exist, God made them
go in cycles. Night comes first, to show how chaotic
things once were and then Day, to show how meaningful
and orderly things now are. Since Day is so much better
than Night, God named the whole cycle after the light,
or Day. The light is therefore called the "dayspring." It
is from this light that the whole idea of "Day" sprang!

And the evening and the morning were the
first day. Genesis 1:5.

Then the LORD answered Job out of the
whirlwind, and said...Hast thou commanded
the morning since thy days; and caused the
dayspring to know his place; That it might
take hold of the ends of the earth, that the
wicked might be shaken out of it? Job 38:1,
12-13.

On the fourth day, God used the sun and moon to
create an earthly symbol of his real days. Therefore like
a photograph of a big city, "earth" days are really just a
tiny earthly souvenir postcard of the original "universe"
days that God made.

And God said, Let there be lights in the
firmament of the heaven to divide the day

> *from the night; and let them be for signs, and*
> *for seasons, and for days, and years: And let*
> *them be for lights in the firmament of the*
> *heaven to give light upon the earth: and it*
> *was so...And the evening and the morning*
> *were the fourth day. Genesis 1:14-15, 19.*

So, God the Creator finished the building of his universe, wrapping things up in six days. He made an expanding universe, which we are just starting to see, using great inventions like the Hubble telescope. Everything was built by the Spirit of God—The Holy Ghost—carrying out God's instructions—The Word of God—and using that glorious first light of absolute vision and understanding—The wisdom of God—to create order and identity to life, and everything that exists.

Because the Creator existed first, and the words and wisdom of all living forms actually came out from him, he is called "Father," and those words and wisdom are his "Son." Now we see why he is called "the Father of lights!" Because the Father, the Son, and the Spirit of truth working together created all life, they all wear the creation action title of "God."

> *In the beginning was the Word, and the*
> *Word was with God, and the Word was God.*
> *The same was in the beginning with God. All*
> *things were made by him; and without him*
> *was not any thing made that was made. In*

him was life; and the life was <u>the light</u> of men. John 1:1-4.

Now therefore ye are no more strangers and foreigners, but fellow citizens with the saints, and of the household of God...ye also are builded together for an habitation of God through <u>the Spirit</u>. Ephesians 2:19, 22.

He that built <u>all things</u> is God. Hebrews 3:4.

Every good gift and every perfect gift is from above, and cometh down from the Father of lights. James 1:17.

The last object God made was a glorious shining memorial home for the architect (God the Father), the building material (God the Son) and the builder (God the Holy Ghost). This memorial's name is "Adam." He is a living, "live-in" 3D photograph of how God works!

God's work—the universe—is expanding, so Adam must expand also, by *multiplying*. Adam's multiplied self is the whole human race! God chose to create Light in the presence of Darkness, so Adam must have the choice to do the same.

And God said, Let us make man in our image, after our likeness: and let them have dominion...So God created man in his own image, in the image of God created he him;

> *male and female created he them. And God blessed them, and God said unto them, Be fruitful, and multiply. Genesis 1: 26, 27-28.*

> *For ye are the temple of the living God; as God hath said, I will dwell in them, and walk in them. 2 Corinthians 6:16.*

But the 3D photograph made a mistake and chose Darkness—Adam chose to exist by a set of instructions not from God, taking away the very reason for his existence. The memorial home had just locked out those who built it! Suddenly, there was no room for God in his own memorial home, and the whole universe groaned and mourned.

> *And the LORD God called unto Adam, and said unto him, Where art thou...Hast thou eaten of the tree, whereof I commanded thee that thou shouldest not eat? Genesis 3:9-11.*

> *And the LORD God said unto the woman, What is this that thou hast done? Genesis 3:13.*

> *For we know that the whole creation groaneth and travaileth in pain together until now. Romans 8:22.*

Ah, where were we? This was supposed to be a glory

story! God the Father, his Son and the Spirit of truth all agreed that the situation was not beyond salvage. The Word and light would come and live in the flawed 3D photograph that was Adam, after taking permission to do so from a small vulnerable piece of Adam, a young Jewish virgin called Mary.

So the mighty angel Gabriel is sent to ask Mary: "Could you please put your life on hold and bring the light of the world into the world to save it? The shining Word is locked out by his own people!" Happily, after a little explaining as to how this would happen, Mary agreed!

> *Fear not, Mary: for thou hast found favour with God. And, behold, thou shalt conceive in thy womb, and bring forth a son, and shalt call his name JESUS. He shall be great, and shall be called the Son of the Highest. Luke 1:30-32.*

> *And Mary said, Behold the handmaid of the Lord; be it unto me according to thy word. And the angel departed from her. Luke 1:38.*

> *Zacharias was filled with the Holy Ghost, and prophesied, saying, Blessed be the Lord God of Israel; for he hath visited and redeemed his people... Through the tender mercy of our God; whereby the dayspring from on high hath visited us, To give light to them that sit*

in darkness and in the shadow of death, to guide our feet into the way of peace. Luke 1:67-79.

Since Adam was the first man, and it was the Word and light's first trip as a man, the Son of God would now become the Son of man. The same builder of all things would set this arrangement up, adding all the new painful, but true details. Adam had locked God out of his home. That painful truth now had to be a part of this glorious story.

So there you have it. We have come full circle and finally caught up with…*and laid him in a manger.* Only the truth of how Adam had no room for God will do, no matter how painful it is, so this glorious story of grace and redemption is told with one little added detail:

…and laid him in a manger; <u>because there was no room for them in the inn.</u> Luke 2:7.

And Jesus said unto him, Foxes have holes, and birds of the air have nests; but the Son of man hath not where to lay his head. Luke 9:58.

Oh, my Lord and my God! This is the radically different vantage point of God's heavenly audience, where anything that shows God's work in the creation story is glory. For these heaven's people, there was no greater glory than when the light came from heaven to save this world's people, and through them, correct and reset the course of the entire groaning universe.

The excitement of the heavenly host at this moment of incredible grace was palpable. I really don't think that the appearance of the large company of angels at Jesus Christ's birth was scripted. I think those angels were so excited and joyful at the dayspring's coming to set right what was wrong that on an impulse, they asked God the Father:

"May we go down there?"

"May we pull back the curtain for just a moment so they can see what's going on up here?"

And I imagine a fondly smiling Father God shaking his head and saying:

"Go ahead, but don't scare them off! And be sure to *wait* until Michael has finished making the official birth announcement before you do your thing!"

And so it was that the formal announcement by a senior angel was suddenly gate-crashed by a joyous party of angels who tore down the heaven-earth partition, singing at the top of their voices to a startled audience of Palestinian shepherds. I may be wrong, but that's how I envision it happened.

> *And there were in the same country shepherds abiding in the field, keeping watch over their flock by night. And, lo, the angel of the Lord came upon them, and the glory of the Lord shone round about them: and they were sore afraid. And the angel said unto them, Fear*

not: for, behold, I bring you good tidings of great joy, which shall be to all people. For unto you is born this day in the city of David a Saviour, which is Christ the Lord. And this shall be a sign unto you; Ye shall find the babe wrapped in swaddling clothes, lying in a manger. And suddenly there was with the angel a multitude of the heavenly host praising God, and saying, Glory to God in the highest, and on earth peace, good will toward men. Luke 2:8-14.

And that is God's version of glory, and the story.

Chapter 24

So, what is glory, really?

Anything that shows God's work in the creation story is glory. To be live-in, 3D photographs of God, our glory *must* tell the story of creation.

The creation story starts off with darkness, chaos and Adam choosing the darkness; therefore we all start with a dark lack of understanding of life's blueprint. We are blind and dead, sitting in the darkness.

> *By one man sin entered into the world, and death by sin; and so death passed upon all men, for that all have sinned. Romans 5:12.*

> *For all have sinned, and come short of the glory of God. Romans 3:23.*

Our next step in the creation story is when we, sitting in the dark suddenly see the light. This is when we are told the truth about the light of the dayspring, and the grace of his coming. His name is Jesus Christ. This is glory.

> *The dayspring from on high hath visited us,*

To give light to them that sit in darkness and in the shadow of death. Luke 1:78-79.

That was the true Light, which lighteth every man that cometh into the world. John 1:9.

And of his fulness have all we received, and grace for grace. For the law was given by Moses, but grace and truth came by Jesus Christ. John 1:16-17.

Our next line in God's creation story is where we literally "step into the light." This choice is only available because the dayspring graciously came as a man to our world. Decide to walk in the light or, having seen the light, decide to stay dead in the darkness—for the first time in creation's story, we get to choose, as God chose. This is therefore the step by which we are *judged.*

The dayspring from on high hath visited us, To give light to them that sit in darkness and in the shadow of death, <u>to guide our feet into the way of peace.</u> Luke 1:78-79.

As it is appointed unto men once to die, but after this the judgment. Hebrews 9:27.

Jesus said, For judgment I am come into this world, that they which see not might see; and that they which see might be made blind. John 9:39.

To walk in the light is to follow the instructions on how to enter and stay in the light—obey the Word of God to get the shining glory-filled wisdom of God. See, the gospel never changes; we've been over all this before! The 3D image now looks like the original. God is light; therefore you are a child of light.

> *God is light, and in him is no darkness at all. 1 John 1:5.*

> *Then Jesus said unto them, Yet a little while is the light with you. Walk while ye have the light…believe in the light, that ye may be the children of light. John 12:35-36.*

Glorious child of light, that's big time glory! But it's time for your next glory step. It's time for you to actually *walk* in the light.

> *Now are ye light in the Lord: walk as children of light: Ephesians 5:8.*

But, how on earth do we do this? Being able to accomplish this feat requires one special choice.

Be a living sacrifice. Yes, become a living sacrifice! Let's break this down to its component nuts and bolts, for us to really understand this.

> *I am crucified with Christ: nevertheless I live; yet not I, but Christ liveth in me: and the life*

> *which I now live in the flesh I live by the faith*
> *of the Son of God, who loved me, and gave*
> *himself for me. Galatians 2:19-20.*

> *Present your bodies a living sacrifice,*
> *holy, acceptable unto God, which is your*
> *reasonable service. Romans 12:1.*

This is a part of glory that we have not previously discussed. It has to do with the dayspring sacrificing his life for all the darkness that followed Adam's choice.

Glory must tell the truth, and the truth of Adam's dark consequence now became a part of the creation story. All that darkness had to play itself out on the dayspring.

So, the Word of light who came as the Son of man to save man must die, carrying all that darkness with him. Jesus Christ was killed by the most disgraceful and prolonged death known to the Romans of that day—crucifixion. That death on the cross was the highest glory of all, higher even, if you can believe it, than his birth!

> *Let this mind be in you, which was also in*
> *Christ Jesus: Who, being in the form of God,*
> *thought it not robbery to be equal with God:*
> *But made himself of no reputation, and took*
> *upon him the form of a servant, and was*
> *made in the likeness of men: And being found*
> *in fashion as a man, he humbled himself, and*
> *became obedient unto death, even the death*

of the cross. Wherefore God also hath highly exalted him, and given him a name which is <u>above every name</u>: That at the name of Jesus every knee should bow, of things in heaven, and things in earth, and things under the earth; And that every tongue should confess that Jesus Christ is Lord, to the glory of God the Father. Philippians 2:5-11.

A good name is better than precious ointment; and the day of death than the day of one's birth. Ecclesiastes 7:1.

Strange, isn't it? You became a child of light through the grace of the dayspring who never gave up on you and laid down his life, first in heaven and then on earth, to save you. Therefore, your walk is worthy only if, through your grace, people in darkness find light as you lay down your life—your wants, needs and material possessions—for them. This is what it means to be a living sacrifice.

This is my commandment, That ye love one another, as I have loved you. Greater love hath no man than this, that a man lay down his life for his friends. Ye are my friends, if ye do whatsoever I command you. John 15:12-14.

Everything I do must be geared towards loving someone else with grace, the way I was loved. This is how I walk in the light! Only then do I support Jesus Christ's ministry of grace. Because the astonishing secret of glory is that it always starts from God's grace! Grace always precedes glory, remember?

The fruit of grace is glory, but glory contains the seeds of grace. For our walk to glorify God we must plant seeds of God's grace in people. This grace grows and bears good fruit in them, fruit which is—more glory!

> *Jesus answered them, saying, The hour is come, that the Son of man should be glorified. Verily, verily, I say unto you, Except a corn of wheat fall into the ground and die, it abideth alone: but if it die, it bringeth forth much fruit. John 12:23-24.*

To glorify God and have that glory multiplied, *I must use my glory to plant new grace trees.*

Chapter 25

Alright, let's get down to commonsense practicalities. How do I glorify God with grace, love and selfless sacrifice all at the same time? This can be broken down into three practical steps.

1. Take our light to the darkness.

The earth was without form, and void; and darkness was upon the face of the deep. And the Spirit of God moved upon the face of the waters. Genesis 1:2.

When Jesus had heard that John was cast into prison, he departed into Galilee... That it might be fulfilled which was spoken by Esaias the prophet, saying... The people which sat in darkness saw great light; and to them which sat in the region and shadow of death light is sprung up. Matthew 4:12-16.

God started creation by facing darkness. Therefore, you must seek out places where darkness lives, where people are not light and the true gospel is not known.

In other words, find places like how you were, before you became a child of light. *Find your Galilee.* Those people desperately need the same grace gift of light that you now have.

2. Declare "Let there be light!"

God said, Let there be light: and there was light. Genesis 1:3.

They that be wise shall shine as the brightness of the firmament; and they that turn many to righteousness as the stars for ever and ever. Daniel 12:3.

This is evangelism or soul winning. That was God's next step and is what happens when you speak the words of light, Jesus Christ! This triumphant start to creating life is worthy of great glory! If you ask God and are willing, the Holy Ghost will show you when to declare light into darkness. This will be startlingly frequent, but remember—you were made for this!

3. Separate light from darkness.

God divided the light from the darkness. And God called the light Day, and the darkness he called Night. Genesis 1:4-5.

Ye are all the children of light, and the

*children of the day: we are not of the night,
nor of darkness. 1 Thessalonians 5:5.*

This is discipleship. We separate the light from darkness by teaching the new light-bearer what is right from what is wrong in God's eyes. We call right "Day," and wrong is called "Night." Naming light and darkness is the only way the new convert can clearly distinguish between good and evil.

When new learners do the instructions of God with the joy and the enlightenment of understanding, they are walking in the light, and are children of light. You, on the other hand, are doing what God did in creation. This whole process, as we now know, is glory.

*And the evening and the morning were the
first day. Genesis 1:5.*

Congratulations! You've just made God's day!

So how does darkness in the world and the universe get cleared away? By the human race, God's 3D photograph, of course! The secret hidden in plain sight is that we are currently living at the time of God's seventh universe day! For us to be in God's image, God had to leave some darkness for us to work on!

God is still at rest in heaven, and his seventh day is full of light. It will never be followed by another night. This means the seventh universe day is the last day God made or will ever make.

> *The works were <u>finished</u> from the foundation*
> *of the world. For he spake in a certain place*
> *of the seventh day on this wise, And God*
> *did rest the seventh day from all his works.*
> *Hebrews 4:3-4.*

The earth becomes the same way after Jesus Christ returns. There are no more days, because there is no more darkness. No more night means no more night-day cycles. The earth joins heaven in the everlasting seventh day of God's Sabbath rest, forever.

> *And there shall be no night there; and they*
> *need no candle, neither light of the sun; for*
> *the Lord God giveth them light: and they*
> *shall reign for ever and ever. Revelation 22:5.*

And what happens to the rest of the groaning universe? Well, this gets quite interesting.

Over at the **National Aeronautics and Space Administration** (**NASA**), scientific calculations using the Hubble telescope indicate that there is matter in the universe which cannot be seen by light, but exists in it. Guess what this matter is called? Dark matter! Dark matter is said to make up over 20% of the universe, by astrophysical calculations.

Is Dark matter waiting for us to declare light and order into it, to fulfill our heritage as creators of light, like our father, God? I think so. I believe this is the only reason God has allowed us know about Dark matter, in these last days. The dark stuff has something to do with us, and our everlasting future.

> *The secret things belong unto the LORD our God: but <u>those things which are revealed</u> belong unto us and to our children <u>for ever,</u> that we may do all the words of this law. Deuteronomy 29:29.*

> *But we all, with open face beholding as in a glass the glory of the Lord, are changed into the same image from glory to glory, even as by the Spirit of the Lord. 2 Corinthians 3:18.*

And away we go, from glory to glory. You see, the picture is so much bigger than we have imagined!

THE JUDGMENT OF GOD

*God shall judge the righteous
and the wicked.
Ecclesiastes 3:17.*

Chapter 26

"**A** Daniel come to judgment! Yea a Daniel! O wise young judge, how I do honor thee!" These memorable lines were uttered by a delighted Shylock in Shakespeare's The Merchant of Venice when, for a moment, an interesting judgment seemed to be going his way.

But for most of us, judgment is not such a friendly word. Judgment evokes images of us standing before a flint-faced judge, in deep trouble, bracing ourselves for a harsh sentence. Yet in reality, much like in Shakespeare's make-believe play, judgment does not always have to be negative.

Think about it. Whenever judgment is served in a court of law, somebody usually comes away happy. Even if no one else is, the lawyers leave happy, especially with the long cases! The key is not to be caught on the wrong end of a judgment. Jesus Christ said as much in the book of John.

> *For judgment I am come into this world, that they which see not might see; and that they which see might be made blind. John 9:39.*

From an observer's perspective, do we all have the same view of judgment? No. From an observer's standpoint, judgment has three perspectives.

The first is the perspective of person being judged. That's the sweating person on the hot seat, the one doing the nail biting. I'm sure we've all been there, at one time or another.

Secondly, there's the judge's perspective. The judge, either literally or figuratively speaking, wears the big judgment robe. From the judge's viewpoint, there must be:

1. A verdict, and
2. A sentence.

To a judge, these two extremely important caveats are what make up a judgment. *There is no judgment if one is present without the other.* Judges usually don't bite their nails; however, when bored, they may spend some time inspecting them.

The third perspective is that of the interested onlooker. Onlookers usually have opinions about who's right, who's wrong and what sentence should be passed. I guess that makes them judges without robes. These "freelance" judges never get bored—if boredom knocks, they quickly resign from the current trial, and find another.

So, why do we ask for judgment? Usually because we have a grievance that we want corrected. Most of the time we have been hurt by somebody and we are left asking questions:

"Why did you treat me this way?"

"What did I ever do to deserve this?"

Our confused hurt hardens into a resolve to have this great wrong righted. And so through judgment, we seek justice. Less commonly and usually not in a courtroom setting, we seek a reward for a person who has done a great good.

Ultimately therefore, judgment is to ensure that good guys get rewarded and bad people pay in such a way that they never do their evil deed again. In other words,

> *We seek judgment to stop evil*
> *and give deserving rewards.*

What is God's perspective on judgment?

The same as ours, as per the final goal! Surprise! God also seeks judgment to stop evil and give deserving rewards.

> *I charge thee therefore before God, and the Lord Jesus Christ, who shall judge the quick and the dead at his appearing... 2 Timothy 4:1.*

> *...For God shall bring every work into judgment, with every secret thing, whether it be good, or whether it be evil. Ecclesiastes 12:14.*

He just has a different way of going about it. We'll look at the differences between God's and man's judgment in more detail in the next chapter.

Chapter 27

We have just said that God and man both seek judgment to stop evil, and give deserving rewards. What then is the big difference between the judgment of God and man?

It can all be summed up in one word. *Love*. Love makes all the difference.

God is love. 1 John 4:8.

There is a story in the Bible of Jesus trying to get to Jerusalem and being barred from taking the shortest route to this city—through Samaria—by a group of Samaritans, for the simple reason that he was going to a Jewish city. At this time there was no love lost between the two ethnic groups.

Jesus' disciples were so incensed by this action that they asked for permission to call down fire from heaven and nuke the Samaritans.

> *He stedfastly set his face to go to Jerusalem, And sent messengers before his face: and they went, and entered into a village of the Samaritans, to make ready for him. And they*

*did not receive him, because his face was as
though he would go to Jerusalem. Luke 9:51-
53.*

*And when his disciples James and John
saw this, they said, Lord, wilt thou that we
command fire to come down from heaven,
and consume them, even as Elias did? Luke
9:54.*

These two disciples were brothers; Jesus had a fond
nickname for them—"Boarneges, sons of thunder."
What do you think Jesus' response was to their fiery
request?

*He turned, and rebuked them, and said, Ye
know not what manner of spirit ye are of.
Luke 9:55.*

God is love.

When a person gets hurt and seeks for judgment,
typically, love is the last thing on their mind. They want
justice, and they want it fast and furious. They want
the perpetrator incapacitated, maimed, killed, or worse
still, damned to hell.

*The person seeking vengeance is a judge without a
robe.* There is no place for love in that person. As the
story above clearly shows, this reckless judgmental
attitude can occur in both people who are righteous and
those who are not.

But *God is love.* This is a very different perspective. I think we understand it better now, after the Glory of God section. That evil perpetrator is a deformed photograph of God, sitting in darkness! God wants nothing more than to have that individual become a child of light. So the Father sent Jesus, the Son.

> *For God so loved the world, that he gave his only begotten Son, that whosoever believeth in him should not perish, but have everlasting life. John 3:16.*

> *For God sent not his Son into the world to condemn the world; but that the world through him might be saved. John 3:17.*

God's approach to judgment is that of a father seeing evil in one of his children. It certainly isn't the immediate response "Nuke 'em!" that we typically would have hoped for. Where would you be if, while you were still in darkness, before you had a chance to change, you got nuked? The bitter truth is that your evil perpetrator was sitting in darkness, *condemned before birth,* long before you ever crossed paths. Once upon a time, so were you.

> *He that believeth on him is not condemned: but he that believeth not is condemned already. John 3:18.*

That condemnation was a hand-me-down piece of clothing from Adam, the first man. The evil person that hurt you so badly has been wearing this straitjacket their whole life! Dark unearned condemnation has colored everything they do.

Now for the first time, that individual can change clothing. They can choose grace, the breathing space that Jesus Christ provides, to stop evil and do good. This is the end result of judgment that both you and God want! But that person's choice will determine the first part of their judgment, good or bad. Because even after seeing wisdom's light, not everyone chooses to follow it.

> *Jesus said unto them, If ye were blind, ye should have no sin: but now ye say, We see; therefore your sin remaineth. John 9:41.*

> *And this is the condemnation, that light is come into the world, and men loved darkness rather than light, because their deeds were evil. For every one that doeth evil hateth the light, neither cometh to the light, lest his deeds should be reproved. John 3:19-20.*

> *Then said one unto him, Lord, are there few that be saved? And he said unto them, Strive to enter in at the strait gate: for many, I say unto you, will seek to enter in, <u>and shall not be able.</u> Luke 13:23-24.*

So God the Father sent us the dayspring from on high, Jesus, so that all people could have a good judgment, and step out of the darkness into the daylight. Or they can continue to sit in darkness, doing evil—their choice! Either way, the first cogwheels of justice have just locked into place. What comes next? We'll see, in the next chapter.

Chapter 28

Grace comes next.

Grace comes, but only if it is not pointless. As we have learned, grace is a statement of God's faith in us. So even though we reject light, so long as there is still a hope, God gives us his grace—time.

We wake up the next morning. And another morning passes by, and yet another. Still, the heavenly host watches and waits. Maybe this is the morning he will change his mind? Maybe she will step out of evening's shame into morning's glory, and glorify God's day?

God sends the Holy Ghost to work on the mind of the flawed individual. The great builder who built everything takes the truth to the part of that person's mind that can still be appealed to. God reveals the truth to them. That conversation, deep in an evil person's mind, goes something like this:

"You know what you did. *I* know what you did! That was not right!"

"Look, I know why you did it, but it is still wrong! Have you considered changing?"

*It's not too late…*you are still here, aren't you? That means you still have a chance! You're still breathing, still standing! If you choose life, I can and will help you!"

"*How* will I fix it? *How*...Child, I'm the great builder; it's what I do! I set up the whole place! Do you really think I cannot separate you from the darkness?"

"There is no evil that cannot be erased in my grace...choose the Day. Leave the fixing to me."

> *Come now, and let us reason together, saith the LORD: though your sins be as scarlet, they shall be as white as snow; though they be red like crimson, they shall be as wool. Isaiah 1:18.*

> *Not by might, nor by power, but by my spirit, saith the LORD of hosts. Zechariah 4:6.*

And so the internal dialogue continues, and all of heaven watches.

Lots of people are changed, and step into the light. Sometimes these individuals are on death row and have almost run out of time. The heavenly hosts heave a huge sigh of relief and shout for joy. And usually, the earthly audience rages:

"It's not fair!"

"Oh, *now* she's found God? What a mind job!"

He needs to pay for what he has done.

But that is only because hurt people look at external appearances and personal history. God looks at the heart.

The LORD seeth not as man seeth; for man looketh on the outward appearance, but the LORD looketh on the heart. 1 Samuel 16:7.

Both God and man want that person to stop the madness. The madness has been stopped, right? This is beautiful in God's eyes! Judgment has been served.

But the story does not always end that way.

A lot of people do not listen to the Holy Ghost's appeal. Unfortunately, this does something to that person. They change by becoming more hardened and a hard-hearted individual is born.

This hardness makes it even more difficult for the individual to be reached by subsequent appeals. The Bible describes this hardening process which gets so bad, that the person becomes as inflexible as stone. There is less space to work with, as the window of opportunity closes, but still God offers grace.

A new heart also will I give you, and a new spirit will I put within you: and I will take away the stony heart out of your flesh, and I will give you an heart of flesh. Ezekiel 36:26.

Finally a tipping point is reached. The evil person has denatured themselves so much that they can no longer change. They have "crossed the Rubicon," the point of no return. It is a different point for different people, but everybody has one, and only your Creator knows when you have reached it.

By a series of consistently bad choices, thoughts become evil all the time. This is the point where for such a person, grace becomes pointless. God, along with all of heaven grieve.

> *And GOD saw that the wickedness of man was great in the earth, and that every imagination of the thoughts of his heart was only evil continually. And it repented the LORD that he had made man on the earth, and it grieved him at his heart. Genesis 6:5-6.*

> *O Jerusalem, Jerusalem, thou that killest the prophets, and stonest them which are sent unto thee, how often would I have gathered thy children together, even as a hen gathereth her chickens under her wings, and ye would not! Behold, your house is left unto you desolate. Matthew 23:37-38.*

God would take away your choice if that would help, but it won't. *You are God's photograph.* God has choice; therefore so must you! Taking choice away defeats the whole purpose of you.

This is the point at which God passes a sentence that will send chills down a grown man's spine. He disassembles that individual.

The spirit goes back to God. The body goes back to the earth from which it was taken. And the soul? It's dead, rubbish without the spirit! It gets thrown into a trash dump called hell.

> *It is a fearful thing to fall into the hands of the living God. Hebrews 10:31.*

> *The soul that sinneth, it shall die. Ezekiel 18:4.*

> *Then shall the dust return to the earth as it was: and the spirit shall return unto God who gave it. Ecclesiastes 12:7.*

Hell's hot. This is God's version of "Nuke 'em!" Judgment has been served.

Chapter 29

So, what is our responsibility in the world today? Don't be a robeless judge! If there is anything the last few chapters have shown us, it is that God has a comprehensive plan for every person's judgment. He doesn't need my special judgment to validate his.

> *Judge not, that ye be not judged. For with what judgment ye judge, ye shall be judged. Matthew 7:1-2.*

> *Vengeance belongeth unto me, I will recompense, saith the Lord. And again, The Lord shall judge his people. Hebrews 10:30.*

When it comes to judgment, this is definitely a case when less is more.

Does this mean we have no part to play in any aspect of the judgment process? Actually, we do play a part—in the verdict.

In the last chapter, the Spirit of God is described as coming to the condemned individual and making the case for change. How does this happen? In most cases, this will be done by God *through other people.* The Holy

Ghost lives in the bodies of righteous people! Being righteous is the same thing as walking in light.

> *Know ye not that your body is the temple of the Holy Ghost which is in you, which ye have of God, and ye are not your own? 1 Corinthians 6:19.*

Children of light are given the unique privilege of making the persuasive arguments that help others step out of darkness. You are the Holy Ghost's mouthpiece! As a child of light you are therefore an agent of God's grace. This is how you will sound:

> *"You know what you did. God knows what you did! That was not right…Have you considered changing?"*
> *"It's not too late…you are still here, aren't you? You're still standing!*
> *…How will God fix it? Brother, the Holy Spirit is the great builder; it's what he does… There is no evil that cannot be erased in God's grace…choose Jesus Christ, the one from who the Day sprang. Leave the fixing to him."*

Wow, people! If I didn't know any better, I'd think I was listening to the great builder himself! You are starting to sound a lot like love to me. But that is the whole idea. As God's living, live-in 3D photograph, that is exactly the way you are supposed to sound.

For it is not ye that speak, but the Holy Ghost.
Mark 13:11.

As God's servants, you will not always be welcomed. On several occasions, you will be accused of being judgmental. No one enjoys hearing the dreaded words:

"Who made you judge? How dare you?"

"Don't you dare judge me!"

These words are just the vicious way Satan and his minions use people to try and shut God's children up. You have judged no one until you have given the verdict a price tag of your own choosing. Don't be intimidated into silence by those harsh words.

Continue to speak up for what is right. God recognizes those who serve him by speaking up for good, in the presence of evil. God will spare you, if his judgment comes to your city.

> *The LORD said unto him, Go through the midst of the city, through the midst of Jerusalem, and set a mark upon the foreheads of the men that sigh and that cry for all the abominations that be done in the midst thereof. And to the others he said in mine hearing, Go ye after him through the city, and smite...but come not near any man upon whom is the mark; and begin at my sanctuary. Ezekiel 9:4-6.*

> *Hurt not the earth, neither the sea, nor the trees, till we have sealed the <u>servants of our God</u> in their foreheads. Revelation 7:2-3.*

This is the part we play in God's judgment process in the world, for now. Leave the sentencing part to God and God alone. But there is a caveat to this. We will discuss this caveat and conclude the judgment section in the next chapter.

Chapter 30

And here comes what seems like the 180 degree turnaround!

Paul says that people *will* judge the world. Jesus told his disciples that they would judge the twelve tribes of Israel. And probably the strangest of all, we are told that we will judge *angels*. Angels?

> *Do ye not know that the saints shall judge the world? 1 Corinthians 6:2.*

> *And Jesus said unto them…ye also shall sit upon twelve thrones, judging the twelve tribes of Israel. Matthew 19:28.*

> *Know ye not that we shall judge angels? 1 Corinthians 6:3.*

What on earth is going on? Hold your horses; there is a very clear reason for this.

In the earlier part of this section, we showed the fundamental difference between God's judgment and man's. The difference is love. This means that if man loves, he judges the same way as God does.

> *We will be allowed to judge when*
> *we have learned to love one another.*

This happens in the kingdom of God.

So we will judge the world—when God's kingdom has fully come in the world. The disciples of Jesus will judge the twelve tribes of Israel—in the kingdom of God. We will judge angels—when God's kingdom comes. All these happen when the kingdom of God comes.

> *Verily I say unto you, That ye which have*
> *followed me, <u>in the regeneration</u> when the*
> *Son of man shall sit in the throne of his glory,*
> *ye also shall sit upon twelve thrones, judging.*
> *Matthew 19:28.*

So when will God's kingdom come? In the future, or is it here already? The answer to both of these questions is *yes.*

The moment we decide to take Jesus Christ as Lord and Savior, we get into his kingdom. It is completely manifested in the person's spirit first which, now being connected to God, simultaneously sits with Jesus Christ in heaven and within the new convert. The spirit knows no distance.

> *God, who is rich in mercy, for his great love*
> *wherewith he loved us, Even when we were*
> *dead in sins, hath quickened us together with*
> *Christ, (by grace ye are saved;) And hath*

raised us up together, and <u>made us sit together</u>
<u>in heavenly places in Christ Jesus.</u> Ephesians
2:4-6.

Therefore, that individual has entered the kingdom of God. This is what Jesus meant when he said that the kingdom of God is within you. It also explains Jesus' statement about the simple, corrupt folk of his day that were getting into the kingdom because they accepted him, ahead of the learned religious ones who did not.

The kingdom of God cometh not with
observation: Neither shall they say, Lo here!
or, lo there! for, behold, the kingdom of God
is within you. Luke 17:20-21.

Verily I say unto you, That the publicans and
the harlots go into the kingdom of God before
you. For John came unto you in the way of
righteousness, and ye believed him not: but
the publicans and the harlots believed him.
Matthew 21:31-32.

But the mind and the body are changed more gradually. The spirit spreads its contained words and light outward, first changing the mind and lastly, the body. And so God's kingdom with the grace of time becomes fully expressed in that man or woman. This is what Jesus meant by the following parable:

> *Whereunto shall I liken the kingdom of God?*
> *It is like leaven, which a woman took and hid*
> *in three measures of meal, till the whole was*
> *leavened. Luke 13:20-21.*

Finally, the light overflows out of the individual towards other people. When two children of light meet, the kingdom of God is seen in a larger measure at that location, because Jesus, the dayspring is there.

> *For where two or three are gathered together*
> *in my name, there am I in the midst of them.*
> *Matthew 18:20.*

In other words, a gathering of the children of light constitutes a slice of God's kingdom here on earth, in the here and now. Among such, there is true brotherly love, as Jesus commanded it should be.

> *This is my commandment, That ye love one*
> *another, as I have loved you. John 15:12.*

Therefore children of light are allowed to judge each other, in love. Like with God, so with his photographs—his people, when in the context of God's kingdom. And that explains the apparent contradiction, highlighted by Paul in his Corinthian letter.

> *Dare any of you, having a matter against*
> *another, go to law before the unjust, and not*

before the saints? Do ye not know that the saints shall judge the world? and if the world shall be judged by you, are ye unworthy to judge the smallest matters? Know ye not that we shall judge angels? how much more things that pertain to this life? 1 Corinthians 6:1-3.

So, to close out the section, let's summarize the judgment of God and our judging responsibilities.

1. God seeks judgment to stop evil, and to give deserving rewards.
2. God judges both good and evil people.
3. God's judgment is always fair, and in love.
4. When in the world, don't judge; rather, express grace.
5. When in God's kingdom, judge one another in love.

And lastly,

If you can't love, don't judge anyone, anywhere!

THE LOVE OF GOD

This is my commandment, That ye love one another, as I have loved you.
John 15:12.

Chapter 31

Love is probably one of the most talked about words, ever. Everybody talks about it in one form or another. It's like a magnet, steadily drawing people into its spell, weaving its way into almost any conversation. So what exactly is love?

> Love: 1. Strong affection for another arising out of kinship or personal ties. 2. Warm attachment, enthusiasm or devotion—Merriam Webster online dictionary.

I think the dictionary got it wrong, this time. There's got to be more to love than that.

You see, I remember frantically leaving work one afternoon several years ago, after an equally frantic phone call from my wife. My then ten-month-old son was running a fever of 104F, and had just had a seizure.

I remember making that twenty-minute trip home in what can only be described as a blur of speed—later, my wife would insist I couldn't have taken more than five minutes to appear.

I remember the tearing sensation in my chest when, on arrival, an ambulance was sitting in my driveway.

Seeing through its rear doors my son, unconscious and jerking uncontrollably.

Later on in the emergency room, the indescribable pain I felt as he had his first urinary catheter passed, screaming the whole time.

You see, "strong affection arising out of kinship," or "warm attachment" doesn't quite cut it for me.

So what is love, exactly? I don't know, not in its entirety. But I can tell you a few things I have learned about it.

I have learned that love is not a feeling. Love is a force. I have come to understand that love is fierce, like a whirlwind, and will blow away anyone that dares oppose its mission—think lioness, and her cubs.

I have learned that love creates strong emotions and tender ones, but does not come from them. After my son's seizure, love made my wife write an article about our ambulance ride that got published in our local newspaper. To this day, my family prays a short prayer every time an ambulance whizzes by with its business lights flashing. We now know what that's like, and love demands action. In fact love insists on it.

> *If ye fulfil the royal law according to the scripture, Thou shalt love thy neighbour as thyself, ye do well. James 2:8.*

Love one another, the royal law of kings.

Love is a royal action word. And since dictionaries cannot define love adequately, and I really don't know what love is, let's see if we have more success looking, not at what love is, but what love *does*. Because, based on everything I have observed and what the Bible clearly has to say, love is so difficult to define for one very simple reason.

God is Love.

Chapter 32

God is Love.

Everything we have talked about until now has been leading up to this. God as love is really *the whole story*. So, let's work our way through the parts of love's story that currently, we can understand.

At the end of the last chapter, we put forward a working model to understand love. We suggested that love is measured by what it does, not how it feels. In reality, love has little dependence on feelings. Rather, love creates feelings, and works *despite* feelings. A simple illustration of this is seen in the joys and woes of parenting.

If your child is sick, you go out of your way to help them. When they annoy you, you angrily correct them. When they perform well in school, you hug them, smiling delightedly. All are examples of love in action, but each is associated with a different emotion.

The first emotion is intense compassion, the second anger and the third, happiness. And don't think for one second that your children don't have strong love-associated emotions of their own. Love makes you do something to help, after you observe a need. Love makes your children act, rightly or wrongly, to achieve what *they* think you need.

Which brings us to what love does. There are two characteristics that are always present wherever love is. It really does not matter which version of love it is—love for a spouse, a dog or an iPad, it makes no difference. If you love somebody, or something:

1.   You want to get to know them, and
2.   You want to help them.

If these two characteristics are not present, I don't care how much you profess otherwise, you do not have love towards that person or thing.

There is a third characteristic which is usually, but not always present.

3.   You want to be around the object of your love.

This third conditional point only fails to occur if being around the object of your love does not help them. This "love from a distance" position is actually quite rare, unless you're some kind of undercover spy, or something exotic like that.

So, in most cases you want to be around your husband, if you love him. Or sit around smiling at your grandmother, if you love her. Or your Smartphone; pick your flavor, it makes absolutely no difference! These rules, simple as they appear, will hold true to any version of love you can think of.

Never forget these love rules! They always distinguish between the counterfeit and the real. If the first two are not present, you are experiencing something, but I can assure you, it is not love! And since God is love, God's relationship with us is summed up using these same rules in the following way:

1.   God knows <u>everything</u> about us.

    O LORD, thou hast searched me, and known me. Thou knowest my downsitting and mine uprising, thou understandest my thought afar off. Thou compassest my path and my lying down, and art acquainted with <u>all my ways</u>. Psalms 139:1-3.

2.   God <u>always</u> helps us.

    God is our refuge and strength, a very present help in trouble. Psalms 46:1.

    I thank my God always on your behalf, for the grace of God which is given you by Jesus Christ; That in <u>every thing</u> ye are enriched by him, in all utterance, and in all knowledge. 1 Corinthians 1:4-5.

3.   God is <u>with</u> us.

    Behold, a virgin shall be with child, and shall bring forth a son, and they shall call his name Emmanuel, which being interpreted is, <u>God with us.</u> Matthew 1:23.

> *Lo, I am <u>with you alway</u>, even unto the end of*
> *the world. Matthew 28:20.*

If we love somebody, we must aim to do exactly the same. The photograph must represent the original. This is as accurate a depiction I know of *what* love does. The *how* of love? We'll look at how love goes about his business, in the next chapter.

Chapter 33

The how of love? This is the look of love, the aspects of love, or love's faces.

Because human beings exist in time, love's goal is to help you through both your present and your future. Remember the words of our Lord Jesus:

> I am with you alway, even unto the end of the world. Matthew 28:20.

Therefore, the "how" of God's love can be broadly divided into two categories, or faces.

1. The short-term how of love—"today," and
2. The long-term how of love—"tomorrow."

The short-term face of love is concerned with immediate needs and wants. Study a person closely, observe their habits and wants, and then provide their want as a gift. God does this all the time.

> What man is there of you, whom if his son ask bread, will he give him a stone? Or if he ask a fish, will he give him a serpent? If ye

> *then, being evil, know how to give good gifts*
> *unto your children, how much more shall*
> *your Father which is in heaven give good*
> *things to them that ask him? Matthew 7:9-*
> *11.*

> *Wherefore, if God so clothe the grass of the*
> *field, which to day is, and to morrow is cast*
> *into the oven, shall he not much more clothe*
> *you, O ye of little faith? Matthew 6:30.*

Now be aware that the two cardinal rules of love—getting to know a person, and helping them—are not broken. They just cater to temporary things. They are the eye-catching acts of love, the ones immediately observed and enjoyed. They are also consumed almost immediately.

So when we give food to the hungry, serve in soup kitchens, organize clothes drives, win a new convert to Christ, volunteer to build for the homeless, wash and wax that new "love" of ours—our new car, we are using the short-term face of love. It is fun while it lasts, which is for *today*. It's here today and gone tomorrow.

> *Today's love satisfies the immediate needs of*
> *the soul.*

The long-term look of love is different.

Tomorrow's love gazes far, far into the future, and is concerned with long-term performance. Most of tomorrow's love works "under the hood," happening in secret, but puts permanent characteristics in place that ensure a great tomorrow. Long-term love doesn't have much of an audience today, but you will be grateful for the help tomorrow.

So when you teach your children how to conduct themselves in public, train people—on your own time—in skills that provide a livelihood, teach table manners, disciple new Christians on God's rules, and take that "love" of yours—your car—in every several thousand miles or so for servicing and an oil change, these are all examples of tomorrow's love.

> *Tomorrow's love satisfies the long-term needs*
> *of the soul.*

The same two cardinal rules of love apply, but in a different way. Long-term love looks for strengths and deficiencies of character. This kind of love shows up mainly as grace gifts, instructions and corrective reprimands.

> *My son, despise not the chastening of the*
> *LORD; neither be weary of his correction: For*
> *whom the LORD loveth he correcteth; even*
> *as a father the son in whom he delighteth.*
> *Proverbs 3:11-12.*

> *For the Father loveth the Son, and <u>sheweth</u>*
> *<u>him all things that himself doeth</u>: and he will*

shew him greater works than these, that ye may marvel. John 5:20.

As many as I love, I rebuke and chasten: be zealous therefore, and repent. Revelation 3:19.

But sadly, this is the face of love that we all too often reject. "Give me today's love! I like it better! Gimme *please...*" we say. And thus, we act as if this was a competition between two totally different loves—today's, versus tomorrow's!

Nothing could be further from the truth.

Chapter 34

Love's faces do not compete against each other! How weird would that be? Who on earth gave us such an idea? I can actually answer that, but won't. This section will not be sullied by his name.

One face of love <u>cannot</u> do without the other.

Furthermore, each face as a standalone entity does not constitute love. <u>*Combined,*</u> they make up one great love! <u>*Together,*</u> they become the one great thing! Let's demonstrate this, using the parent-child relationship once again.

If all you did was give your child treats, candy and whatever they felt they needed "today," but did not teach them how to dress, personal hygiene, did not teach them subjects in school to prepare them for adult responsibilities in the future, did not teach them *anything at all,* as you "lovingly" plied them with pies, cakes, candy and toys. What kind of adult would that child grow up to be?

We have just created a self-centered, obese, unemployable, very unkempt, very, very smelly person. And that is putting it mildly.

Not so good, huh! Well let's try tomorrow's love.

If all you did was give instructions and bark out correcting reprimands to your child. No hugs, no treats, no kisses, no fun rides, no giggling play in the park, as you severely but "lovingly" train them on all the rules, proverbially (and/or literally), rapping their knuckles every time they break them. What kind of adult will that child grow up to be?

We have created an adult who, for better or for worse, has just survived child slavery! Does "timid nervous wreck" or "crazy rebel" come to mind, as possible outcomes here? Talk about putting the "fun" in "dysfunctional," only that wouldn't be fitting, because that poor child had no fun!

That's what happens when the two faces of love are separated. But we know this stuff already! A similar warning is issued in this well-known idiom:

> *All work and no play makes Jack a dull boy;*
> *All play and no work makes Jack a mere toy.*

The faces of love are one.

Because God *is* love, we unfortunately make the exact same mistake with him.

We have created the mean Old Testament God, whom we have called God, the Father. And we have come up with the loving, cuddly New Testament God, whom we have called Jesus Christ, God the Son. But the Son that we have cherry-picked as the loving God is an exact replica of God his Father!

Philip saith unto him, Lord, shew us the Father, and it sufficeth us...John 14:8.

Jesus saith unto him, Have I been so long time with you, and yet hast thou not known me, Philip? he that hath seen me hath seen the Father. John 14:9.

God, who at sundry times and in divers manners spake in time past unto the fathers by the prophets, Hath in these last days spoken unto us by his Son, whom he hath appointed heir of all things, by whom also he made the worlds; Who being the brightness of his glory, and the express image of his person...Hebrews 1:1-3.

God the Father and God the Son are one. When you have seen one, you have seen the other. But we want to love today's God only, and have little time for tomorrow's God. This is clearly seen by the things we say and do.

Out of the abundance of the heart the mouth speaketh. Matthew 12:34.

The most popular modern Christian praise songs heard in our churches today express love for today's God, talking about all the treats he has given us. But personally, I do not recall hearing a modern praise song that expresses our delight in God's long-term love plan in a long, long time.

The last one I can clearly remember is "Trust and Obey"—written in 1887! But the Psalms of David, a biblical collection of praise songs, repeatedly pay tribute to both aspects of God's love very well.

Wouldn't it be great if our praise and worship songs were balanced in our regard of God's "today" and "tomorrow" love? Then our songs would sound like psalms. We'll end this chapter with a sampling of what those old praise songs had to say.

> *I have been young, and now am old; yet have I not seen the righteous forsaken, nor his seed begging bread. Psalms 37:24-25.*

> *I will delight myself in thy commandments, which I have loved. Psalms 119:47.*

> *The LORD is my shepherd; I shall not want. Psalms 23:1.*

> *Blessed is the man whom thou chastenest, O LORD, and teachest him out of thy law. Psalms 94:12.*

> *I have longed for thy salvation, O LORD; and thy law is my delight. Psalms 119:174.*

Chapter 35

Well! That's an awful lot of info on love! Not bad, for not really being able to define the word! Maybe we should recap what we have learned so far:

> Love must know about me.
> Love must attempt to help me.
> Today's love brings gifts, to satisfy me today.
> Tomorrow's love brings instructions, to satisfy me tomorrow, and
> Today's love cannot live without tomorrow's.

I think that captures most of the highlights, so far. So, how do I use all this information, in my day-to-day living?

> *Thou shalt love the Lord thy God with all thy heart, and with all thy soul, and with all thy mind. This is the first and great commandment. And the second is like unto it, Thou shalt love thy neighbour as thyself. Matthew 22:37-40.*

Here, Jesus divides love into the love of God and the love of neighbor, but indicates they are both one. We will follow the same method, discussing the way we experience love in relation to people and to God, as two parts in the same chapter.

PART I – PEOPLE.

1. I can now discern true love from people.

It would appear that I can tell whether I am truly loved or not by a person, by simply going down the five-point checklist from the beginning of the chapter. Are they interested in me? Are they trying to help me? Do they bake me pies one day, and firmly correct me when I'm wrong the next? See, this is easy when you know what to look for!

The flip side of that coin is I can pick out the fakes too. Do you flash a broad smile at me all the time, but never help me in any way? Do you even smile at me *at all*?

Do you talk about God, but never really remind me of him? Are you always tomorrow's instructor, but never today's gift-bearer? Or, conversely, are you *always* today's gift-bearer, but *never* tomorrow's instructor? Why do you always act so busy when I'm around? Did you just poison my pies?

Anyone who thwarts the things that would bring me glory is poisoning my pies. God cannot be glorified through me if I am not glorified; I am his photograph! Anyone who refuses my grace seeds poisons my pies. My grace from God cannot abound toward you, if you keep turning down my love gifts!

> *Remember the words of the Lord Jesus, how*
> *he said, It is more blessed to give than to*
> *receive. Acts 20:35.*

I help you all the time, by accepting *your* love
gifts! Why are you trying to rob me of my blessing, by
rejecting mine?

2. I can learn to give true love to people.
This is not inherent, though some people have an
advantage here, either from their genes or their job. But
let us not kid ourselves; everybody could get a lot better
at this! This means for me to love you:

> *I must make an effort to get to know you.*
> *I must always try to help you.*

The cardinal rules of love need to constantly be
on my mind. I understand that it goes against our
natural inclination, which is toward self-centeredness.
However, for some of us, we can apply these rules easily
with the people we know we should love—our children,
parents, best friends, siblings etc. But what happens
when we meet somebody we do not know? Or worse
still, someone who does not wish us well at all?

> *I say unto you, Love your enemies, bless them*
> *that curse you, do good to them that hate*
> *you, and pray for them which despitefully use*
> *you, and persecute you; That ye may be the*

children of your Father which is in heaven.
Matthew 5:44-45.

A training program we instituted in my house identifies somebody during the course of each day that is outside of our circle of family and friends. We really were not able to identify any family enemies, so we decided strangers were the next best thing. We then pray specifically for this individual, during our evening family prayers.

By this technique, you are forced to concentrate long enough on a virtual stranger to identify something about them that stimulates prayer. You are getting to know more about them! Your prayer helps them! Your observation could be of good or bad; it really doesn't matter. This has worked well for my family as a first step in radical love training. I hope it works as well for you as it did me. As I said before, we all could use some help in this area!

Another technique is of eating out in a restaurant once a month or so, with a special mission in mind. No, it's not what you are thinking! This is not for you, bright-eyed steak lover!

This is for someone else. Pick somebody or a family within view or earshot distance, and buy them a whole or part of a meal. No questions asked, no glory sought, but make sure you observe them long enough to get a feel for what they may like. In other words, don't buy a vegetarian family fried pork chops!

I'll share one more love technique with you. Actually, it's my favorite one! I had an enemy for a brief period (he is an enemy no more, thanks to this maneuver!) I don't know how it happened, but it just did. You know how that goes.

He kept saying bad things about me and my quality of work behind my back. People started coming up to me and telling me the things he was saying. After a particularly insulting remark he had made, I made a decision.

I will buy him a gift.

So, I went to the gift shop at work and looked around, asking God the whole time "Please help me find something for this man!" I avoided the bunnies and flowers in bright pink wrapping paper—they didn't seem appropriate, and I'm not in the habit of starting something I cannot finish. And then I saw it.

A single pocket-sized diary, tucked away all by itself, on a shelf. In it were questions on each day about how you felt on that particular day, or about a wide array of topics. It gave a few suggested answers, in a multiple choice format, to choose from.

This was perfect! I excitedly went up to the pay register, but the elderly lady behind the counter was puzzled, because she could not find that diary anywhere in the store's inventory! Also, it had no price tag on it! After several minutes, she asked,

"How much do you think its worth?"

"Hmm, maybe…$7.50?"

"Okay then. That will be $7.50, sir!"

And so I paid for it, and picked up a peanut butter granola bar from the cafeteria on the way back upstairs…he looked like a peanut butter kind of guy. And as these things have a way of working out, I ran into him almost immediately, as he sat down at a computer terminal close to mine.

I wish you'd have been there to see his face when I gave him his diary! It was priceless! And while he was still reeling from my straight right cross,

"What kind of granola bar do you prefer—oatmeal or peanut butter?"

Dazed pause. "Peanut butter. Why?"

It was time to finish him off.

"I *knew* it!" Gleefully, I dug into my coat pocket and offered the granola bar.

"I got this for you."

And with that I bade him good afternoon and casually strolled away.

Left hook…Lights out! That was several years ago. As you probably have guessed, I haven't had a problem from him since.

> *Be not overcome of evil, but overcome evil with good. Romans 12:21.*

Give thoughtful gifts to people who persecute you. It disarms them.

PART II – GOD.

1. I can now discern true love from God.

I have been told that God loves me. How do I know this? By going down the same checklist, from the beginning of the chapter!

God certainly wants to know about me! This is seen by his statements all through Holy Scripture. One of the first steps used in getting to know somebody is you visit them at home. You learn all kinds of details about a person by observing them in their own home. So, God visits you at home.

> *They heard the voice of the LORD God walking in the garden in the cool of the day... And the LORD God called unto Adam, and said unto him, Where art thou? Genesis 3:8-9.*

> *And when Jesus came to the place, he looked up, and saw him, and said unto him, Zacchaeus, make haste, and come down; for to day I must abide at thy house. Luke 19:5.*

But if you really love somebody, you want to be around them as much as possible. So you go more frequently to their home for more prolonged periods— "hanging out at the crib," the sleepovers, even the long Skype calls—and their house rapidly becomes your second home.

Understanding this, how much do you have to love a person that you want to live in their house *forever*, if they will let you? I'd say you'd have to love them a mind-boggling amount, wouldn't you?

> *If a man love me, he will keep my words: and my Father will love him, and we will come unto him, and* <u>*make our abode*</u> *with him. John 14:23.*

> *God hath said, I will dwell in them, and walk in them; and I will be their God, and they shall be my people. 2 Corinthians 6:16.*

God really, truly loves me. There's no other explanation for a deep level of intimacy like that.

God is totally invested in helping me! This is why God gave his son Jesus Christ as a sacrifice, so that I could be saved. When he gave us Jesus, God the Father gave us everything he had! He has nothing left to give, nothing left to say for our redemption.

> *For God so loved the world, that he gave his only begotten Son, that whosoever believeth*

in him should not perish, but have everlasting life. John 3:16.

For God sent not his Son into the world to condemn the world; but that the world through him might be saved. John 3:17.

But that is not all. God the Son gave up everything *he* had and died for me! Jesus had all kinds of glory in heaven that he gave up. Given what he gave up, he died first to his heavenly house before he completed his death, in the earthly home of his physical body. Unfathomable, radical—there are really no words to describe a love like that!

I live by the faith of the Son of God, who loved me, and gave himself for me. Galatians 2:20.

And yet it doesn't end there! God the Holy Ghost comes and lives with us, serving us eternally, directing and helping us forever! The great builder of the universe, chooses to live in and serve—*me?* That is the nature of the God we serve.

2.   *I can learn to give true love to God.*

We are now gurus of the two cardinal rules of love. Therefore to love God, I must want to get to know him, and I must want to help him. Anything other than that does not qualify as love, no matter how I spin it! So I have to find a way to achieve these two goals.

How do I get to know God?

I get to know God by spending time with him. This is done by listening to God's words—through the Holy Bible as well as quiet contemplation, and talking to him—in prayer and praise, followed by...more quiet contemplation!

You have to read your Bible! It is spiritual food for your starving spirit. You normally eat everyday, don't you? Read and/or contemplate God's words everyday as well. You will become familiar with God's likes, his dislikes, his mannerisms and habits so that when you hear words that are his, you will immediately be able to say—that is the Lord!

> *Blessed is the man that walketh not in the counsel of the ungodly...But his delight is in the law of the LORD; and in his law doth he meditate day and night. Psalms 1:1-2.*

> *He said unto them, Cast the net on the right side of the ship, and ye shall find. They cast therefore, and now they were not able to draw it for the multitude of fishes. Therefore that disciple whom Jesus loved saith unto Peter, It is the Lord. John 21:6-7.*

Prayer is a conversation with God—in his language. Praise songs are when you sing your half of the conversation. But it takes two to converse. After your singing, it is time to be quiet, and listen to what God has to say in response.

Be still, and know that I am God. Psalms 46:10.

God's answer is usually heard during your quiet time of contemplation.

How do I help God?
I help God by doing his commandments. His commandments are any one of his instructions. Now I have spent time with God, I know what he likes, and I can now do those good things. This is where my fear of the Lord training kicks in. I do whatever God asks me to do, because the things God asks me to do are the things he likes!

If ye love me, keep my commandments. John 14:15.

In this the children of God are manifest, and the children of the devil: whosoever doeth not righteousness is not of God. 1 John 3:10.

But of all the things on God's wish list, what is most important to him? What does God want for Christmas? There's really only one thing right now that makes God's heart beat faster, and you are looking at it, when you look in the mirror.

You.

God loves people! Loving God is choosing to love what God loves—you, and your fellow man! I believe that you cannot love God that you cannot see, if you cannot love the people in the world that you can see! God is very clear on this point of loving one another. We are *commanded* by God to do it!

Therefore I am first and foremost, a gatherer of people for God, at the personal sacrifice of self—my time and resources. I cannot say I love God without it!

> *These things I command you, that ye love one another. John 15:17.*

> *Hereby perceive we the love of God, because he laid down his life for us: and we ought to lay down our lives for the brethren. 1 John 3:16.*

> *For he that loveth not his brother whom he hath seen, how can he love God whom he hath not seen? 1 John 4:20.*

Loving God and my fellow countrymen should be a lot easier now, after all we've talked about in this section, I hope! But make sure you are demonstrating your love, not just talking about it. This is a time when talk is cheap. Talk less and love more!

> *My little children, let us not love in word, neither in tongue; but in deed and in truth. 1 John 3:18.*

How many times have you watched a movie where the bad guy tells the trapped hero all about his grand scheme, and after he has spilled his guts, he never gets to carry out the grand plan! He'd have had better luck if he'd acted first, and talked later! Come on folks! Love God and brethren first, and *then* talk about it!

So there you have it. These suggestions may or may not work for you, but I'm sure you can come up with more novel ways to love people, if you think about it. You're smarter than you think! The God part though is pretty much mandatory. But whatever you do, make sure that whenever you meet people, you are looking at them through the lens of love!

DAY ONE

That was our final conversation.

For the seeking believer, I hope you learned about God's kingdom, and the part you play in it. The seven conversations are as follows:

> "So what exactly am I supposed to do now?" *Hearken unto me: I will teach you the fear of the LORD.*

> "Who is Jesus Christ exactly? I mean, really?" *Christ the power of God, and the wisdom of God.*

> "God, it's hard to walk with you. Every step seems to get me rejected by the world!" *Peace I leave with you, my peace I give unto you: not as the world giveth.*

> "I don't think I'm good enough for you, God. I'm too flawed." *My grace is sufficient for thee.*

> "Okay, I'm finally becoming somebody! What comes next?" *Fear God, and give glory to him.*

"Will I also be judged, now that I've gotten my act together?" *God shall judge the righteous and the wicked.*

"Sometimes I just don't know how to show my love for you, God. How do I show you my love?" *This is my commandment, That ye love one another, as I have loved you.*

"Is that what you really want, God? If I do it, will you love me then?"

I have always loved you.

The ultimate goal of my love for you is that you live your life and become the very best "you" there is! I want to share your transformation, helping you along your glorious journey. I want to be there, gleefully sharing with you your splendor, at your glorious end.

So I ask you to fear me, so that I can help you. You don't understand it now, but you'll love me later. Do my word and get my wisdom. It's the only way.

Catch my peace.

Remember, everything I gave you was an unearned gift. Never forget the grace from which you came.

Go ahead, reach up…stretch! Reach down and help somebody reach up. Look at you child…just look at you! Now it is done. All is glory!

You have finally learned to love me, like I love you.

ACKNOWLEDGMENTS

This has been a whirlwind of a book! But no worries! I have had the privilege of writing about what is, for me, the most important topic of all.

Thank you Heavenly Father, for sharing your kingdom with me. I am incredibly privileged to have been given such an assignment by you to complete. Once again, I hope I have done you proud.

Thank you Jesus Christ, my Lord, Savior and King. I cannot wait to I see you face to face, but until then I cherish the opportunity to capture your living essence with the written word. Your look of love is what keeps me alive and gives me the strength to write about you.

Thank you Holy Spirit! You have honored this broken "God home" with your presence and made me whole again. Thank you for the wisdom of your guidance. You reveal my Lord Jesus to me today, with whispers of ancient yesterdays.

Thank you Debrah, my wonderful wife and spiritual "wind." You are always my first editor. Words cannot express how grateful I am for your love in action.

Thank you, Samuel, Daniel and Emmanuel. You boys make me smile. I see God's kingdom in you, guys. I love you.

Thank you Pastor Vincent Windrow! Brother Vinnie, your wise input on this book's portrayal of God's kingdom is cherished and highly valued. On a more fun note, your energetic sermons are frequently reenacted at home by my sons.

Thank you Sue Reed so much for your input on editing, done in record time! I hope the next one is a little slower. Mum, I owe you big!

And lastly, thank you Pedernales Publishing, for your elegant work on both eBook and hardcopy. But then, I would expect no less. God bless.

CPSIA information can be obtained at www.ICGtesting.com
Printed in the USA
LVOW11s2057021113

359709LV00001B/1/P